Cliff Parker has wri[tten] on the
subject of fishing for many years. *The Fishing
Handbook to End All Fishing Handbooks* and
Hook, Line and Stinker are available from
Sphere. He now writes for the *TV Times*.

The Compleat Wally Angler

CLIFF PARKER

SPHERE BOOKS LIMITED
London and Sydney

First published in Great Britain by
Sphere Books 1984
30–32 Gray's Inn Road, London WC1X 8JL
Copyright © 1984 by Cliff Parker
Cartoons © 1984 by Graham Allen

Set in Century Schoolbook

Printed and bound in Great Britain by
Cox & Wyman Ltd, Reading

Contents

The Compleat
Wally Angler

Introduction

The word *wally* has been in common currency for several years now, but of late its use has escalated to include all kinds and conditions of men. So common has it become, indeed, that a worried W. Bennett wrote to the *Birmingham Evening Mail* to complain about it.

'Why is it that wally is a derogatory term?' he asked plaintively. 'I have been a Wally for over 63 years and never do anything stupid.'

It is possible that Mr Bennett got hold of the wrong end of the stick. How can wally be a derogatory term when there are so many of them, outnumbering nonwallies in almost every field of activity?

To be a wally is to be IN. And it's not as easy as it looks. Some wallyskills come naturally, but many more are acquired only after years of practice.

The origin of the word is lost in the mists of time, but it is almost certain that it originated in angling. Of all activities, angling offers the most scope. Just look at the factors involved, unique in leisure pursuits:

You are out in the open air, with total freedom from domestic or professional constraints.

You are hunting in an alien environment – i.e. water – for an invisible and cunning prey. (Invisible and stupid, actually, but we'll let that pass.)

You are using specialised tackle, of the utmost delicacy, but with lethal possibilities.

You are handling baits of the utmost indelicacy, but with just as many lethal possibilities.

1

You can dress as you please.

You can either hunt alone, or in the company of dozens – even hundreds – of like-minded sportsmen.

The stress involved in this apparently soothing pastime means that at the end of the day you are generally in need of some kind of sedative. If you've not been supping all day, that is.

*   *   *

The Father of Angling, Izaak Walton himself, was among the earliest of wallies, known as one by name as well as nature. Doubtless there were Comrades of the Angle who hailed with, 'Hello there, Ikey!' But it is almost certain that he preferred to be addressed as Wally.

There is a variety of European gherkin known commonly as a wally. As sold in supermarkets and delicatessens, it is small, thick-skinned, green and pickled: which description fits exactly the wallyangler who lurches off coach or boat after a hard day's battling with the elements.

So what exactly is a wallyangler? That's the question this book sets out to answer, with full instructions on how to achieve wallydom. Just to get you started, here are some examples:

Wallies make their own floats. Lots of people do that, but wallies make them at three times the cost of shop-bought floats, not counting the bill for re-surfacing the dining room table.

Those floats which do not sink at first cast, stand proudly six inches out of the water at half-cock. By the time enough shot have been added to get them standing at full-cock, and only three inches out of the water, there are few fish around with enough weight or muscle to make any impression on them.

Wallies tie their own flies. So far, not a single wallyfly has made the Hardy catalogue. There is obviously a reason for this: perhaps the fact that a wallyfly looks like something from *The Muppets Meet the Wolfman,* and its only effect on a fish is to frighten it to death.

They take the fly-tying very seriously and use traditional materials: sheep's wool gathered from hedges; gamecock hackles; fur from a hare's ear. When these are in short supply or over-expensive, they turn for substitutes to sources nearer home. It is possible to identify an underprivileged wally fly-tier by the state of his pets: an alopecic cat and bald budgie are dead give-aways.

Wallies stuff their own fish, and the result is always an improvement on nature. Size, for a start: where on the Grand Union Canal could you find an eleven-inch gudgeon? Colour, for a second: it will liven up the freshwater angling scene no end when bright orange pike are commonplace, but so far they can be seen only on a wally's wall.

Where he does fall down a little on his stuffing technique is in the shape. By the time he's finished skinning, curing, stretching, stuffing and losing bits, the fish looks a little less than aquadymanic. The only way it could swim would be in ever-decreasing circles, a sure progression towards extinction.

Wallies get excited on the bank. Every successful strike is greeted with cries of, 'Omygawd! It's huge! Look at that rod bend!' It's a bit of an anti-climax when the six-ounce perch is finally reeled in.

At the opposite end of the scale from the innovators are the Creatures of Habit. There are wallies who have fished the same stretch of canal, rain or shine, every week for thirty years, using the same tackle and the same bait. No use telling Tradwally that nothing's been caught on cheese there for a quarter of a century; that the outfall from the radiochemicals centre killed every fish in the stretch twenty years ago; or even that there's been no water in the canal since it was drained. That canal and those methods were good enough for his dad, so they're good enough for him. His dad never caught anything, either.

3

Many wallies overdo the Demon Drink *before* they get to the water, instead of after, and often find their favourite spot a bit quicker than they intended by marching 101 yards down a 100-yard field. A river in flood carries many strange floating objects with it: uprooted trees, hen houses, cattle troughs and the occasional unwary cow. A strange floating object wearing wellies and a surprised expression is likely to be an over-fortified wally.

Not that all wallies are ensnared by the Demon Drink. Many of them are teetotalwallies. Such a one is the committeeman who holds up proceedings in the angling club by fussing over every point of procedure. It matters naught to him that the bar closes in ten minutes. He is often surprised when his hands are trapped in the drawer so that he can't vote against the motion for adjournment.

*   *   *

The foregoing examples are but a few, and give only the merest idea of the range of wallyangling. The rest of the book will fill you in; allow you to develop wallyskills to match your own circumstances, pocket and personality.

It won't always be easy, but persevere. Just remember that a thing worth doing is worth doing well. That mony a mickle maks a muckle. That Rome wasn't built in a day. That every cloud has a silver lining. And that many hands make light work.

If you can go around remembering wallythings like that, you're well on your way...

Instant Wallyskills

Although it can take a lifetime of hard work and dedication to become a really top wallyangler, there are many things you can do to achieve instant wallyness. Check with this list of just some of them: you might be surprised to discover how many you're doing already.

Running a lap of honour along the bank with every fish over three ounces, clutching the fish in your hot little hand in case anybody wants to admire it.

* * *

Painting your rod with a high-gloss varnish so that people will notice you're fishing with quality tackle. A lack of success means the fish have noticed, too.

* * *

Tightrope walking across a lock gate in the dark after a club social.

* * *

Squeezing your groundbait into a tight ball and using a high trajectory to get a better splash.

* * *

Seeing how far you can throw the fish back at the end of the day. Livens 'em up.

*   *   *

Elbowing your way into the crowd around a hotspot and casting right next to the bloke who was there first.

*   *   *

Noting all pre-baited swims the night before and getting down there first next morning.

*   *   *

Slinging eels into the undergrowth when they don't count in a match. Great for the image of angling: especially in front of the TV cameras.

*   *   *

Improving your groundbaiting skills by practising with your catapult. On ducks.

*   *   *

Dealing with a pike in the old-fashioned way, i.e. panicking madly, kicking it up the bank and stamping all over it. Only language they understand.

*   *   *

Blowing raspberries during the club secretary's annual speech every time he mentions the honoured guests from the rival club. Occasionally making the same noise with your mouth.

*   *   *

Dapping under the rod tip for a big chub through a tangle of hawthorn and briar at the bottom of a six-foot vertical bank. Get out of that...

*   *   *

Slinging 30 lb of groundbait into your swim to hold the fish. When the total muster in the half-mile stretch of canal couldn't eat it in a week.

*   *   *

Getting rid of your surplus maggots on the way back from a match by tipping them down the back of the coach seats. (Not recommended if you're likely to get the same coach next week).

*   *   *

Waiting until the team has left the coach for a hedgeside pee and shouting 'About TURN!' at the approach of another coach bearing an outing from the Ladies' Temperance League.

*   *   *

Playing a fish with the ratchet on the reel so that everybody knows you've got something.

*   *   *

Reeling in with the ratchet on when you haven't got a fish so that everybody *thinks* you've got something.

*   *   *

Reeling in with a ratchet clogged with sand, in case anybody along there is deaf.

*   *   *

Diving in for a swim at the end of your session. So the others haven't finished fishing yet? So, tough...

*   *   *

Flicking a pike spoon at the ear of another boat angler who's fishing too close. Relying on your customary accuracy tolerance of six feet either side. Which fails you. The case comes up on Monday.

Dedicated Followers Of Fashion

It's not always enough just to *be* a wallyangler: you've got to be *seen* to be one. And the best way of doing this is to adopt one of the wallyangler's instantly recognisable guises.

As your wallying skills improve and your personality asserts itself, you can add all kinds of individual touches to your outfit; perhaps even invent a new wallygarb altogether which will catch on among the eager initiates around you. Boy George did it, dammit, with a few discarded Christmas wrappings and some Oxfam rejects, and look at him now.

Don't delay! Start today! And to help you on your way, here are some basic wallyangling outfits. One of them is bound to be *you*.

CASTRO'S CAST-OFFS

In search of the true butch image – the real hard man, used to living rough in the wide open spaces – you could do no better than try the Castro's Cast-Off look. Very popular with underweight bank tellers, building society counter-clerks, self-service garage cashiers, computer programmers and supermarket till attendants, who would rather be Charles Bronson, Clint Eastwood, Telly Savalas, or just about anybody.

It involves little attention to personal hygiene in the morning, neglecting as you do to shave, clean your teeth, or even wipe the sleep out of your eyes. Did Zapata ever do that? The time you save can then be devoted to climbing into your gear.

Lace-up shooting boots, unzipped flying boots, fur freezer-boots or turned-down waders; camouflage trousers; old and cracked flying jacket or leather bomber jacket. For your head there's a choice of a Basque beret, baseball cap, bush hat or postman's peaked cap. The postman's cap may not sound very exciting, but, squeezed in at the sides and pushed up at the front, it gives the authentic and menacing look of a redundant Latin American police chief. Whatever headgear you choose looks more effective if worn with a fringe of long and greasy hair.

Somewhere around your middle, strap on a four-inch wide black leather belt with a buckle announcing that it was once the property of Wells Fargo, Che Guevara or Wild Bill Hickok.

You're kitted out now, except for the knives. Carry at least two: one stuck down your right boot, the other slung from your belt. All good wallytackle shops offer a choice of everything from a machete-sized Bowie to a thin and wicked-looking Swedish filleting knife. Neither of which would you know how to use, but that's not the point, is it?

Now you're ready for off. Affect the authentic bandy-legged walk of the hardened bandito, not difficult if you're wearing a low-slung Bowie knife. Carry your baskets slung either side so that the straps look like crossed bandoliers, and carry your rods in a hold-all like a slung rifle. Give menacing glances through narrowed eyes to any old ladies you meet on the way, and twirl your moustache if you've got one. If you haven't got one, a little Cherry Blossom boot polish will provide you with an instant Groucho job. You can't twirl it, but you can leer under it.

The overall image affects not only old ladies, who tend to throw palpitations at the sight, it also affects young and nubile girls, who tend to throw up on the spot.

Don't carry the hard-man act too far. If the bailiff asks why, in the absence of membership cards, you are not even wearing your club badges, don't reply, 'Badges? We don't need no steenkink badges!' He might throw you off the bank and you'd be very upset, having to sit around with nothing to do but suck your thumb and wait for the next *Sierra Madre* audition.

NOW YOU SEE HIM...

The Invisible Wally is a common sight by the water, or he would be if you could see him. Otherwise known as the Camouflaged Kamikaze, he's the one with the Hawkeye complex; the invisible hunter stalking his prey silently and unseen through the undergrowth.

To accomplish the disappearing trick, you kit yourself out at a government surplus shop with a camouflage battledress, bush hat and a yard of green netting. The netting you drape over your head and decorate with bits of twig and foliage.

To make sure that nothing reflects any light through the net, you darken your face with burnt cork, mud or cowpat. In the absence of hat, net or hair, do the same thing to your bald head. Take out your false teeth. Either remove your spectacles or paint them with anti-flash liquid or a coating of mud or cowflop. To ensure that you can see, mark a cross in the middle of each lens with a matchstick.

Toothless and half-blind, you can now make your way to the water secure in the knowledge that you are absolutely invisible to the fish.

The technique has its drawbacks, though. In your purblind state, you could pack up after an exhauting day's angling to find you've been fishing the M6.

Another drawback is that you are not only invisible to the fish, you are invisible to everyone else, or at least in a state of camouflage sufficient to have you mistaken for a deformed tree or a heap of tangled vegetation. This condition renders you liable to all kinds of accident. Very few Invisible Wallies finish a day's fishing unscathed; many, indeed, are scathed beyond repair.

The least that can happen is a thorough dampening of the spirits by a succession of wandering dogs. It's bad enough sitting there with your trousers all soggy, but with the taller or more ambitious dogs, you're really in trouble. Do not attempt the camouflage in a safari park, by the way: with giraffes or elephants, you wouldn't stand a chance.

Courting couples in search of a bit of privacy are often disconcerted when the tree under which they are plighting their troth gives out with a polite, 'Ahem!'. The less understanding among the swains are liable to assuage their embarrassment by kicking the tree up the bole.

Even first love has its dangers. Instead of getting straight into the action, the shy young wooer may pass the time by carving a set of initials and a pair of hearts entwined. You could try closing your eyes and thinking of England, but generally you can't hold out much above Wolverhampton.

Normally harmless wildlife can do a lot of incidental damage. Shortsighted woodpeckers, squirrels in search of autumn nuts, hedgehogs looking for a hollow in which to hibernate: all can take your mind off the fish and have you leaping about, screaming for a tree surgeon. Not to mention undernourished Dutch elm beetles, which in force can leave you with a nose like an antique cheese grater.

And if somebody walks along and chalks a cross on your bum, followed in the middle distance by a bloke lugging a chainsaw, it's definitely time to pack it in.

The Invisible Wally technique has been tried over hundreds of years, but seldom without complications setting in. The most famous, and possibly least success-ful, was Thomas Birch, 18th-century scholar, enthusiastic but hopeless angler and Wally Extraordinary.

So keen was he to catch something that he made himself a full-length tree outfit, with branches for sleeves and knotholes in the trunk to see through. All dressed up, he waddled down to the bank and started to fish. Not only did he not catch anything, he was rendered extremely soggy by wandering dogs and embarrassed by friends who picnicked all around him. It was not so much the picnicking that upset him as their asking, 'I wonder where that silly old bugger Birch has got to today?'

The Camouflaged Kamikaze is even more liable than any of the other eccentric dressers to give heart attacks to old ladies on public transport. Down-and-outs (see following wally) and Mexican desperadoes they can cope with - but triffids are just too much.

A LONG SMELT WANT

For the real back-to-nature wally, there's nothing to beat Worzel Gummidge's scruffier brother, of whom it is often said that he keeps coming back like a pong.

This is for the knowledgeable wally who once read somewhere that fish are allergic to the taste or smell of soap. So at weekends you take very good care not to use it.

Superstitious and a great believer in tradition, you refuse to have anything done to render your fishing outfit habitable by a normal human being. Your lucky socks were those in which you won the club individual trophy in 1967, and you have never had them tubbed since. The lucky long johns took you to a victory in the needle match of 1973, and since then never have they felt the action of an enzyme. Your pullover, alas now severely holed by the depredation of moth and continual scratching through years on the bank, saw you only just miss the top weight in '75. Or was it '74? And your Irish tweed thornproof trousers are held together at the flies by a series of safety pins. So what? Where can you buy a pair of trousers like that these days? And who makes zips strong enough to hold 'em?

So attired, you make the odd bob or two on the way to the water from old ladies and well-meaning clergymen who press some small coin of the realm into your grubby mitt and implore you not to spend it on the Demon Drink. If nothing else it will cover your fare on the bus, on which you seldom have trouble getting a seat – or several seats – to yourself.

At the water, you indulge in a few odd habits, such as the old matchfisher's trick of keeping maggots warm under your tongue on cold days. Keeps 'em lively, you see. The fact that they turn comatose as soon as they hit the ice-cold water is neither here nor there.

Instead of packing a conventional lunch, you nibble happily at whatever bits of old cheese are lurking about among the fluff and fag ends in your pockets. As a result of this you are never much in demand for giving the Kiss of Life to victims of accidents on the bank. That's a pity: one blast of the foetid mixture of Sainsbury's time-expired cheddar, warmed-through maggots and Augustus Barnett scotch is enough to waken the dead, though a second blast would restore them to their original, i.e. defunct, condition.

Animals on the bank show no fear of you, in fact are strangely attracted, perhaps because you do not smell like the dreaded enemy, Man, but more like a heap of maturing compost, the bilges of a dredger or a sewage farm clearance sale.

It is annoying to conventional anglers that, in spite of an aura that could bring a rhino to its knees at ten yards, you still manage to catch fish. It would be a very suspicious fish indeed which associated the flavour of a skunk on heat with any threat to its wellbeing.

The fact of catching fish in spite of it all might affect your standing as a qualified wally if it were not for your insistence on joining in the socialising after a fishing session.

When any number of anglers are gathered together in a pub, there is a swift and inevitable build-up of fug. But your contribution out-fugs the lot.

You get to the pub damp, as does everybody else. But you've got a lot more to offer than the run-of-the-mill auras of mud, weed, slime, canal water, fish scales, maggot skins, scotch and cheese-and-pickle butties. You have *Pong X*, the dreaded angling wallypong that can make strong men turn pale and trainee barmaids buckle at the knees.

Pint of brown-and-mild in hand, you head for the fire and plonk yourself foursquare in front of it, close enough to perish the rubber on the backs of your wellies. But the burning rubber has difficulty in getting itself smelt over what fills the air once you start to warm up.

If there's foul weather outside, your fellow anglers are forced to stay in the bar, shuffling outwards from the fireplace into an ever more tightly-packed ring. All the landlord can see is a press of steaming bodies, through which emerges a thickening fug which is doing his mynah bird no good at all. He can't see you, marooned as you are by the fireplace, so he attributes both pong and fug to collective responsibility.

'Drink up, please!' he shouts. 'Well past time!' When there's still half an hour to go. And he makes a mental note to have a 'No Anglers Allowed' sign painted before next weekend.

It's no use arguing with landlords like that. Leave with dignity, letting him know that you've been thrown out of better pubs than his. Comfort your fellow ejectees with the opinion that it's an ill wind which blows nobody any good, and that the landlord probably watered his beer anyway.

Do not be upset, or even surprised, if your sentiments fall on deaf or even hostile ears; if you are picked up by your brothers of the angle and dumped into the nearest water butt or thrown into the canal. It's the price of principle that every true pioneer ought to be prepared to pay.

Pretty Boy Wally is far from invisible. Not that he's flashy. Nor, like the wallyhusband (see 'All in the Family'), is he dressed in colours bright enough to scare anything more perceptive than a gudgeon with its head in the sludge. But in the average crowd of anglers he stands out like a beacon, simply because he's neat and tidy, and scrupulously clean. All of which are very wally things to be, because this is not what angling is all about.

Oh, it's not, eh? Perhaps not to the bunch of scruffs you are forced to call your clubmates. But *you* have standards of sartorial elegance and personal hygiene to uphold.

You may well have started your fishing career as an Eager Beaver (see 'Ourselves When Young'), and in adult life have managed to stay uncorrupted by the appalling standards of dress and cleanliness of those around you.

It is not a case of your Nearest and Dearest pushing you or nagging you into a smart turnout. *You* are the fastidious one, and it's as much as she can do to have a freshly cleaned and pressed outfit ready for every fishing trip. Not that it matters if she can't: you are just as much at home with the steam iron and stain remover, and often prefer to apply the finishing touches yourself.

Knife-edged gaberdine slacks, immaculately cut windcheater over a matching rollneck pullover. Sturdy but fashionable brogues for summer fishing; neat olive-green wellies or lace-up shooting boots for the winter. A rakish cap or tweed fore-and-after to keep the wind from your immaculately groomed hair. A couple of badges, perhaps, but no more. Never the profusion of the wallybadger (coming up). Just a discreet Milbro, Abu or Mitchell label, depending on the colour match, neatly sewn on the left breast or on the front of the cap.

You are in great demand by the committee for presentation to visiting dignitaries as a typical member of the club. While the really typical scruffy and drunken rabble are being held at bay, you are produced to make small talk and tell Sir Humphrey how eternally grateful you and the rest of the club are for being allowed to fish on his land.

Sir Humphrey is very impressed, as is his lady wife, to whom the sight of a genuine typical angler would prove distressing, if not fatal. The distinguished pair go away quite happily, with a totally false impression of what's roaming the river on their estate, and the club's fishing concession is safe for another year.

The fact that you fish all day, often in inclement weather, does not mean that your immaculate appearance of the morning is in ruins by the end of the day. You finish the session as neat and clean as you started it, a phenomenon which ranks among the Great Unsolved Mysteries of Angling.

Nor, in spite of your concern to keep your clothes unsullied, do you fail to catch fish. You do consistently well, recording catches that keep you well up in the individual weights, despite the hint of aftershave in your groundbait.

All in all, you're a credit to any club. An object lesson in dress and deportment, personal hygiene and sober habits. Held up as an example by all club wives to their scruffy, smelly and intemperate spouses.

Do their scruffy, smelly and intemperate spouses show you the respect you deserve? Do they attempt to change their ways of living and mode of dress to follow your example? Do they hell.

They mutter in corners of the bar about Little Lord Fauntleroys, jammy buggers and bloody fairies. At the annual prizegiving ceremony they greet your present-ation (for Outstanding Services) with wolf whistles and cries of, 'Hello, sailor!'.

Take no notice. It's just their fun. Their comradely way of expressing grudging admiration and affectionate envy. They don't *really* hate your guts. Honest, they don't. But just watch it next time you're crossing a lock in the dark.

You've been everywhere, man. And you've got badges to prove it. Cloth badges, metal badges, plastic badges, stick-on badges, iron-on badges.

You've used every make of tackle, too, as your decorations testify. What's more, you've fished in every important match, series and festival since records began.

It does cause the odd bit of confusion at away matches, when name tags are being worn, and the opposition match secretary introduces you as 'Mr Mitchell ... er ... Mr Milbro ... Mr Abu? No ... Mr Leeda. Or is it Mr Daiwa? No ... silly me ... Allow me to present Mr Shakespeare.' After that, Sid Wally is a bit of a comedown.

And the places you've been ... Miami ... Palm Beach ... Mississippi ... Bangkok ... The Great Okeefenokee Swamp ... Morecambe ... They're all recorded on your person. You've not actually been to *all* the places yet. Morecambe was very nice, though. Death Valley, California? Not a lot of fishing there, surely? Not since the Pleistocene Age, no, but it's bound to come back one of these days.

Closer inspection reveals your vast range of activities and amazing mobility. In one week alone you were fishing in the British National, the Florida All-Stars Marlin Championship, the Texas Bass Knockouts, the Blackpool North Pier Festival. You were also ski-ing like a good 'un in the downhill slalom in the winter sports at North Island, New Zealand.

Still closer inspection reveals your bravery in two world wars, demonstrated by the awards of the Military Medal, the Croix de Guerre and the Iron Cross. Not to mention donating 4,750 pints of blood, winning a bronze for the Veleta in 1929, completing the 75-yard breast-stroke and running off with the Prix d'Honneur from the 1976 International Black Pudding Championships.

The profusion of colours in the cloth badges does no harm on the bank; even helps, in fact, by providing a first-

It gets you noticed, dunnit?

class camouflage. When a fellow angler has difficulty in making out what's underneath it all, what chance does a fish have?

But the effect is ruined by the clatter and flash of the metal badges, especially when those on the hat have been augmented by gleaming silver spoons and iridescent spinners. Even a fish, dim though it is, realises that somethings's wrong. It's not every day you have camouflaged lighthouses clanking up and down the bank, especially ones that have difficulty in standing up.

Still, it gets you noticed, dunnit? When you walk into the pub, everyone wants to look at your badges. When they've had their bit of fun, that is: springing to attention, shouting, 'Stand by your beds!', giving a Wolf Cub salute, chanting, 'We dib-dib-dib!', singing a rousing chorus of 'Gooly-gooly-gooly-gingangoo . . .' and asking if they can play with your woggle.

Sense of identity. That's what badges are all about. Showing you Belong. Expressing your personality.

A quick skim through the labels reveals that you are an honest-to-goodness schizophrenic. That you belong to a worldwide fraternity of exhibitionists that knows no frontiers and ranges from pearly kings and drag queens to Latin American dictators. That you are a fully qualified and practising wally. And what's so wrong with that?

When they've had their fun, when they've run out of corny jokes and tasteless wisecracks, and when you've finished your pint, leave the pub with dignity. They're only jealous. Nothing better to do than take the Mickey.

Climb into your car which, like yourself, is highly ornamented; the doors decorated with Snoopy Dog stickers, the windows plastered with pennants announcing, *I've been to Pontin's, Skegness is so Bracing* and *It's Better in Blackpool*. Reverse out of the car park with care: a high proportion of badge enthusiasts end up backing straight into the water. Not only is it difficult to turn around in the driving seat when you're encased in an outfit stiffened by a hundred pieces of embroidered canvas, but there's a window sticker which obscures the fact that the bank sweeps in sharply just outside the car park exit. It's usually the sticker that says *Happiness is a rod in your hand.*

Ourselves When Young

You're never too young to start practising your wally techniques. Indeed, it is at the outset of your angling career that you can begin the specialisation which determines what kind of a wally you will be when you grow up.

Junior wallies are divided into two main types: the Eager Beavers and the Snotty Grotties. Both are equally detested by adult anglers, even by wally adult anglers, and it is from the adults' treatment of them that the youngsters derive the complexes which serve them so well in later life.

Eager Beavers take the whole thing very seriously from the start, read the angling encyclopaedias from cover to cover and back again, do the same with all the angling magazines, and join junior clubs with Baden-Powell-type names such as Albatross, Cormorant, Fish Eagle and the like.

Their tackle is extensive, expensive and immaculately kept. Their outfits are always brand-new, immaculately tailored and spotless. Some of them have rich fathers who provide all this. Others earn it themselves through such out-of-school enterprises as delivering newspapers, working on milk rounds, cleaning cars or mugging old ladies.

They are usually loners, often because they want to give all their concentration to the catching of fish and prefer to keep their techniques to themselves. But mainly because other kids can't stand them.

Your Eager Beaver technique starts with the approach to the bank in copybook style: bending low, keeping off the skyline and crawling silently to a likely spot. The likely spot is next to an adult angler: not close enough to be an official nuisance, but close enough to make him aware of your presence and to feel uneasy about the professional and muted goings-on upstream.

Your preparations are methodical and unhurried, setting up the keepnet and landing net before anything else. You take the temperature of the water, test the depth precisely along the length of the swim, note the action of every little current and eddy, mark the positions of underwater obstructions or potentially useful features such as weedbeds.

You groundbait skilfully, dropping some of the stuff into the eddy just upstream of the muttering adult, allowing enough to drift down to draw off any fish he may have collected around him.

Then you start pulling the fish in, striking expertly with a flick of the wrist on your boron rod, playing them only as long as is necessary, and drawing them over the landing net smoothly and without fuss.

This happens every five minutes or so, and finally your adult neighbour, peeved at his own lack of success, offers you some friendly advice, such as, 'Why don't you bugger off?'

Eager Beavers are noted for their politeness and correctness, so you answer gently, 'I'm sorry, sir, but I'm fishing at the recommended distance from you, as I'm sure the bailiff will confirm.' This will often shut him up, as the bailiff would doubtless also confirm that he hasn't got a ticket.

Eager Beavers are noted for their helpfulness, not to say know-all attitudes, so you continue:

'If you don't mind my saying so, sir, you are groundbaiting far too wide an area. If you were to use less bait and concentrate on the edge of that weedbed, I'm sure you'd do better. And I see you're using paste. You'd be far better off on maggot.'

'Why don't you mind your own sodding business?' is your neighbour's avuncular response before he lapses into *sotto voce* comments such as, 'Bloody kids. Bloody cheek. When I was their age. Bloody mollycoddling. Don't know the half of it. National Service. Do 'em the world of good. Never did me any harm...'

But his groundbaiting technique changes and, turning his back to you, he replaces the paste on the hook with a couple of maggots. Ten minutes later you hear his calm and assured screams of, 'Strike! I've gottim! Omygawd!'

Helpful as ever, you lay down your rod, walk up behind him and offer helpful and constructive advice: 'Don't panic, sir. Keep your rod up. Now put some sidestrain on. Don't shove the net under him like that, sir. You'll spook him. Slide the net into the water and draw him gently over the – Oh dear, you seem to have lost him. If only you'd...'

It is at this point that you feel a resounding 'Boi-oing!' on your left ear and see the multi-coloured lights flashing before your eyes. It is now time to pack up and move further upstream, settling down next to another adult angler. Not close enough to be an official nuisance, but close enough...

Snotty Grotties have much more fun. Their approach to fishing is highly unscientific – indeed, fishing is only part of the whole day's enjoyment – and their effect on adult anglers is far more devastating than the polite irritations of the Eager Beaver could ever be.

The Snotties are pack animals, for a start, roaming the bank in droves in search of fun and excitement, giving vent to such traditional angling chants as 'ARSEnal! ARSEnal!' or 'LiverPOOL! LiverPOOL!', and following up with, 'Tott'nam, Tott'nam, we will kill you! *Kill you...*'

Little loves.

Harrassed by a troop of homicidal midgets...

To begin as a Snotty Grotty you have to pay far more attention to your appearance than the conventional Eager Beaver. The hair has to be cropped close enough to look like the aftermath of a bad attack of nits. You may be lucky enough to have a low forehead, which helps immeasurably towards the overall Missing Link effect. Should your forehead not naturally be low, don't despair: it will soon get flattened from continual use as an offensive weapon during your outings with the Junior Football Hooligans Club.

Your footwear is sturdy and serviceable: a pair of fourteen-eyelet Doc Marten's or well-studded industrial boots for preference. Above them you wear a pair of half-mast, paint-splashed and custom-torn jeans, and top these off with a bomber jacket decorated with loo-chain epaulettes and a tasteful array of swastikas on the back.

You are not yet old enough to be allowed into a tattoo parlour, but you have done the best you can with transfers and a ballpoint pen, decorating your arms with symbols and sentiments that gave the Third Reich a bad name. There's plenty of surface area for experiment; your arms hanging, as they do, well below your knees.

Your approach to the water is rather less stealthy than that of the Eager Beaver. There is often a stile or five-bar gate to be attended to first. You and your mates spend five or ten minutes vaulting over or tightrope-walking along it before you tire of the fun. After which you demolish it, set fire to it, or wrench it from its hinges.

On the walk across the field you may encounter some cows, bullocks or sheep. It is incumbent upon you to chase these around the field a couple of times, out of the gate if you can manage it, and on to the motorway slip road if it's not too far.

But these are only diversions. A little light relief before the serious business of the day. Which is . . . Wot is it? Oh, yer – fishin', innit?

Down the slope to the bank charges your merry throng. Turning cartwheels, and fighting along the way, slapping cowpats in each other's faces, belching and farting as descant and counterpoint to the football chants, and kicking around empty cans of Coke and 7-Up.

Though you and some of your friends have kitted yourselves out to the best of your ability, there are those among you who are scantily equipped or who have no tackle at all. So at the bank the throng splits into smaller groups, each led by the lucky lad who's fully tackled-up, and each group heads for a separate and solitary adult angler.

With the polite greeting of, ''Ello, mister. Nobody sittin' 'ere, is there?' and totally ignoring any kind of answer, you plonk yourself down five feet away from him.

'Got any bait I could borrow, mister?' you ask politely. Upon his reply in the negative, your mates yell, 'Yer! Course 'e 'as!', scramble down the bank and relieve him of a handful or so of maggots, with socially relevant comments of 'Miserable old git...' and 'Skinny old bleeder...'

The angler takes no retaliatory action. Because of your revolting appearance and aggressive behaviour, he is not sure whether he is on *Candid Camera* or being harrassed by a troop of homicidal midgets.

Sling in your line, as opposed to casting it out, in the very spot being fished by the angler. The flatiron weights cause a great splash as they hit the water, rocking his float and sending a wash right back to the bank. When you're really proficient you will be able to hit his float and cross his line nine casts out of ten, but that is a skill which comes only with practice. Have patience.

Attempt to engage him in friendly conversation, just to show there are no hard feelings:

'Wotcha got, mister? Anyfink good?'

His reply is inaudible, so you try again. But all you can make out from his mumblings are sentiments implying that he would wish to see you in a state of total disorientation after first having received personal attention from a taxidermist.

27

This churlish behaviour is too much for your stalwart comrades, who by now anyway are thoroughly bored with kicking cans up and down the bank. They descend on the angler's keepnet and haul it from the water, to disclose the shaming truth that its contents are no more than a couple of stunted gudgeon.

'Yah! Silly old git!' they chant. 'We caught *millions* bigger'n these last week!' They emphasise the point by whirling the dripping keepnet round their nitty little heads, drenching the angler and giving the gudgeon severe vertigo.

The angler, who was gentle Jeykll when you arrived, now turns suddenly into horrifying Hyde. Snatching a rod rest from the bank, he leaps among your little friends and belabours them unmercifully, caring no more whether they are homicidal midgets or not.

At this point your float dips and you haul out a huge fish, which stands no chance against your hawser line and butcher's hook.

'Look at this, mister!' you call to him, hoping that the true comradeship of the angle will set in at the sight of your monstrous catch. But all it does is to throw him into an even wilder paroxysm of rage. Perhaps because it's the local monster he's been trying to catch all morning.

There is little for it now but to disappear at top speed and find another angler to pester: there's no shortage of them on a good day. And perhaps you or one of your mates will come across an older brother along the bank – the one with the tattooed knuckles and German helmet – who will gladly, in the interests of brotherly love, stop kicking the old lady anti-vivisectionist and do the same to the miserable old bleeder who's been so nasty to you.

Good, fishin', innit?

Bending The Elbow

There has always been a close connection between angling and the Demon Drink. The very word 'angle' comes from the Greek, meaning 'elbow' or 'that which is bent'; thus confirming the connection between fishing and elbow bending at least as far back as Ancient Greece.

The Latin word for fish, *piscis*, is another indication. Do we not to this day describe a man in a state of alcoholic intoxication as *pisced*? The implication being, of course, that he has just returned from fishing.

Izaak Walton himself was never out of the boozer for long, as his writings indicate. Not only was he always heading for the pub, he was also constantly trying to lure innocent passers-by and complete strangers in after him.

And so has grown the tradition of the wallyangling club, where the boozing has usurped the original intention of a day out. Or has it? Was boozing always the original intention, with the fishing thrown in for cosmetic effect?

Whichever came first, the fishing or the supping, it's the wallyclub you must seek if you are to gain maximum enjoyment from your activities. To help decide which club offers the best potential, ask to see the logbook of the outings. A typical wallyclub log should run something like this:

0700 Coach arrives at pick-up point, the *Clog and Muffler*.

0730 Coach finally loaded: a couple of crates per person and several bottles of the sterner stuff. Oh, and fishing tackle.

0830 Coach arrives at setting-down point, the *Rampant Ferret*. Members, rating as bona fide travellers, have a few winter warmers in the private bar, and stock up coach again before setting off to the water. Those that *are* setting off.

0945 First anglers arrive at the water, settle themselves down and have a swig or two of the hard stuff to keep out the cold.

1045 First cast.

1046 First casualty: one member hooked in the ear.

1047 Second casualty: one member in water. Knocked there by member whose ear he hooked.

1052 Peace restored. Everybody drinks to that.

1100 Pubs open. Members retire for short break.

1500 Pubs close. Short break still in session.

1520 Members ejected, kicking and struggling.

1530 Members invited, by affiliated drunk, to visit local angling association, whose bar has a club licence.

1800 Members invited to leave local angling association, after supping the bar dry. Not to worry; the pubs are open again.

1810 Back in *Rampant Ferret*, after assurances to landlord of best behaviour on the part of all concerned.

1845 Ejected from *Rampant Ferret* after small misunderstanding involving landlord's wife and tin of maggots. Third casualty; treated for contusions caused by bar stool wielded by landlord's wife.

1900 Members gain entrance to the *Galloping Gudgeon* by counterfeiting utmost sobriety.

1945 Ejected from *Galloping Gudgeon* after facade of sobriety cracked. As did several pint pots over members' heads. Casualties four to eight; slight cuts and mild concussion.

2000 Coach arrives to pick up party.

2030 Coach moves off after being loaded with crates from off-licence up the road.

2130 Coach arrives back at *Clog and Muffler*. Ninth casualty: knocked down steps in rush for bar.

2215 Outbreak of fisticuffs, occasioned by accusations of boasting and fibbing, quelled by landlord. Casualties ten, eleven and twelve: various missing teeth.

2300 *Clog and Muffler* closes. So?

2345 Members ejected from *Clog and Muffler*. Thirteenth casualty: foot stuck under brass rail.

0130 All but one of members make it home. Casualties fourteen to thirty-five: mainly cases of severe battering by next-of-kin.

0730 Remaining member returns home. Mates had propped him up at wrong house. Thirthy-sixth casualty: not expected to recover for some time.

* * *

With a report like this, it looks as if you've found your club. Try to avoid becoming the thirty-seventh casualty.

Some Side-Splitting Wallyjapes: 1

One of the hallmarks of the true wally angler is his highly
developed sense of humour and his endless capacity for
practical jokes. Nothing like them for spreading cheer
along the bank; for livening up what could otherwise be
just another routine outing.

And there's no sport like angling for providing
situations and raw materials for some truly side-splitting
wallyjapes.

Angling offers the classic ingredient for a true horror
story, for a start; one that Hammer Films missed, but one
which was used to fantastic effect on telly in the *Doctor
Who* series – MAGGOTS!!!

Puke! Groo! Yuk! Bleargh! What more could a wally-
japer want?

Maggots slipped into your mate's sandwiches are
always good for a laugh. Make sure they're clean, though:
don't want to give the game away because bits of sawdust
get stuck between his teeth. And it's not half the fun if you
let him eat all the sandwich before you break the news.
Let him eat half of it and *then* tell him. Just watch his face
as he peels back the top layer of the remaining bread to
find all those revolting little creatures squirming about.
Tee-hee.

For the full shock effect, bed the maggies down in
mayonnaise: there's nothing like an oily yellow medium
to help the little chaps realise their full throw-up
potential.

Have your camera ready to capture the sequence of events – disbelief as you break the news; shock-horror-bleargh as he peels back the top slice. The third action in the sequence is often difficult to capture on film, as it's either a king-sized fist heading for your gaily-laughing countenance, or the rest of the butty being stuffed down your trousers.

Which brings us to the disposal of surplus maggies at the end of the day. If you don't want to take them home, especially if they're on the turn, say casually to your mate, 'Look up there! Isn't that a flying saucer?'

As he cranes his neck to the sky, pull out the waistband of his trousers and tip the contents of the tin down inside. That's generally good for a full ten minutes' screaming and leaping about the bank; even, if you're lucky, the spectacle of his dropping his trousers and scrabbling about panic-stricken inside his Y-fronts. It also gives you time to collect your gear and disappear.

* * *

Don't worry when your maggots chrysalise into casters. You can have some great fun with these by mixing them with your mate's pipe tobacco. With the casters you can also mix in some well-matured bran or sawdust from the bait tin: it all adds to the flavour.

Don't go away. You have to be around to enjoy the discomfiture – i.e. the uncontrollable throwing-up – of your mate as he lights his pipe. At the very first puff there is a series of sharp explosions and your mate takes in a lungful of smoke smelling strongly of barbecued blue-bottles and well-matured horses' doovers.

You can doctor his cigarettes, too, using the blunt end of a baiting needle to make a tunnel into the tobacco, pushing in three or four casters and teasing the tobacco back over the hole.

Be ready with some appropriate wallyquips such as, 'By heck, those cigs seem to have a high protein content', or, 'Are those King Size, Kong Size or Pong Size?'.

Your mate will no doubt take it all in good part and you will soon gain a reputation on the bank as a Bit of a Wag. Just in case he does not take the joke in the spirit in which it was intended, you'd better learn to swim.

* * *

The official nonwally method of maggie disposal is to take the surplus ones home and pour boiling water on them. It's instant and painless – at least, nobody's ever had any complaints – but it's not all that convenient and it does take some of the fun out of things.

For simple convenience, just chuck the maggots into the swim at the end of a session. This ensures that the fish which have kept well away all day will come cruising up for a feed, deserting other swims and leaving the anglers wondering why the bites have suddenly stopped.

Or just sling them on the bank. In seconds they will have disappeared, maggots having a fair turn of speed once they put their minds to it. They will re-appear again in a couple of weeks as bluebottles and, having taken a liking to that bit of bank, will hang around in clouds to plague whoever's sitting there. That's a highly entertaining spectacle for a start. Unless it's you who are sitting there, in which case it's not funny at all.

You can use the maggots in the pub, tipping them down the blouse of any girl who takes your fancy, as a demonstration both of your affection and your highly-developed sense of wallyhumour.

Sometimes the shock is enough to send her into an impromptu striptease, ripping off her blouse to the immense enjoyment of all wallies present. And if she merely fumbles at her cleavage in an attempt to locate the things, it's your chance to use your rapier-like wit and ask if she wants a hand.

If, at that moment, her seventeen-stone boyfriend emerges from the Gents and proceeds to re-arrange your features, do not forget that you've read this disclaimer:

*In the event of your features being re-arranged
by person or persons, known or unknown, of
whatever size, shape or weight, neither the
publishers nor the author of this book can
accept responsibility.*

In other words, serves you right. You should have
checked first.

. . . After such an outbreak of wallyfun, it is likely that
the landlord will intimate he would rather you took your
custom elsewhere, emphasising this polite intimation by
throwing you out.

You may just have time, before his hand descends on
the scruff of your neck, to dispose of the remaining
maggies unseen down the backs of the seats or under the
cushions. This will ensure a plentiful supply of bluebottles over the coming weeks and possibly a visit from
the brewery's area manager or the sanitary man.

The landlord may be peeved for a while but, once the
pub's been fumigated, he may well see the funny side of it
and laugh heartily. Or he may not: some people are not
over-endowed with a sense of humour. Who needed that
pub, anyway?

* * *

Among those who do appreciate a little wallyfun is your
wallymate. Once he's got over the maggots in his butties
and down his trousers, and the casters in his tobacco, he'll
be looking forward to more jolly japes. So for him you can
prepare little surprises such as a tin of surplus maggies
left in his garage. After a week or two he will notice it,
wonder what it's doing there, and take the lid off to check
the contents.

Anybody was has seen a swarm of bluebottles leave a
bait tin will subscribe to the theory that the legend of

Pandora's Box was inspired by an ancient Greek wally poking around his garage.

And if your wallymate can take a joke, so can his loving wife. For her you leave the maggies in the fridge, in a Tupperware box labelled 'Long Grain Rice', which maggies in a comatose state so closely resemble.

They will cause quite a sensation when she serves them at the next at-home for her friends in Weightwatchers, having, as they do, such a delicious nutty flavour when boiled. Not that anybody should complain, either – maggots being almost 100 per cent protein – but you know what some people are like.

A Glossary Of Wallyangler Terms

Fought like a tiger.
   The fish twitched twice in twenty-five yards.

A fine-conditioned fish.
   It only had one eye, but at least all its fins were intact.

The fish on that water don't give themselves up.
   You didn't have a nibble all day.

The fish refused to feed, no matter what I did.
   *You were fishing by the bleach outfall, just fifty yards
   downstream of the local hotspot.*

Fought hard and long.
   *It was at least thirty seconds before it rolled belly-up
   and died.*

Evaded me at the net.
   *You bashed it on the head with the rim of your landing
   net. Upon which it jumped and broke the line.*

A monstrous pike.
   Two and a half pounds.

Crafty fish... kept stripping the bait.
   You struck too late.

Sucked the bait clean without a tremble on the float.
The float bobbed wildly for thirty seconds but you didn't notice.

Had the most incredible bad luck. Still, it could happen to anybody.
The luck consisted of fifty bites, twenty strikes, three hookings and two line breaks. Happens mainly to total incompetents.

The bank was quite overgrown.
You snagged your line on the only tree for 400 yards.

My wife encourages me to go fishing. Says the fresh air is good for me.
Your wife can't stand the sight of you/is having an affair with the milkman. Possibly both.

My speciality is the long-distance cast.
You keep snagging the trees on the other side of the canal.

My speciality is accuracy. I can drop my bait on a 5p piece.
Once they make 5p pieces with a diameter of fifty yards.

I don't believe in all this fine-and-far-off rubbish.
You've only got an old river rod with a set in the tip and you can't cast more than five yards.

I make all my own floats. Must have a couple of hundred by now. Got my special favourites, of course.
Only three of them don't sink at first cast.

A little feathered lure I tied myself. Unconventional but deadly.
A green-and-ginger weighted monstrosity, bearing a close resemblance to a New wave bog brush, whose

deadliness is dependent upon its braining a surfacing fish.

No fancy gear for me. Tried-and-trusted, that's the thing. Keep it simple.
You've only got two floats.

I was not at the peak of my form.
You were pissed.

The man's a complete show-off and his methods ought to be investigated.
He catches more than you.

The man's an absolute incompetent. Couldn't catch a starving piranha in a bucket.
He catches slightly less than you.

Show me any water and I'll find the fish.
You could catch a starving piranha in a bucket.

A close-fought finish to the match.
The winner had a total of 151lb 3oz. You had 3oz.

I've had extensive experience of waters abroad.
You fell in a canal outside Calais and once had a day in Yorkshire.

The continentals will weigh in anything. Bloody tiddler-snatchers.
The French match team snatched the tiddlers you couldn't.

My club secretary thinks I stand an excellent chance of fishing for the 'A' Team.
Providing the other fifty candidates for a place meet sudden death or total incapacity before Thursday.

Always a lot of antagonism in the 'A' Team. I wouldn't care, but it comes out in such sneaky, underhand ways.
Your team mates keep sticking your feet in buckets of quick-setting cement and throwing you in the canal.

In top-flight match circles, you're only as good as your last catch.
You were dropped from the team after building up an aggregate of 2 oz, 3 drams over the past six months. Your last catch was the back of the match secretary's neck. He was not impressed.

I always buy the best. Lasts for ever and it's cheaper in the long run.
You've been using the same hook all season.

Groundbait additives. That's the secret. I've got a formula I wouldn't sell for a thousand pounds.
You chuck some custard powder in.

It was a big 'un all right. Just over an ounce short of the record. But luckily the line held
The 3 oz gudgeon failed to smash the 4 lb line.

Interesting pike on the wall there. I had one just a few inches shorter not so long ago.
Thirty inches shorter. In 1963.

But when it comes down to it, there's nothing like the blue marlin. Out in the old Caribbean.
You read a book by Hemingway once.

I fished steadily on until 11 o'clock.
The pubs were open.

All of a sudden, the fish stopped biting.
The pubs were open.

I can't recommend that pub. Doesn't cater for anglers.
You'd fallen in the water and slipped on some farm-fresh cowpat. The landlord was quite tolerant until three regulars exhibited signs of terminal methane poisoning.

Ditto
The landlord refused you admittance after you fell over the step, passed him an empty scotch bottle and said, 'Fill her up'.

Ditto
The landlord threw you out after you dropped a handful of maggots down the barmaid's blouse. How were you to know she was his wife?

Ditto
At the George and Dragon the fierce lady behind the bar demanded, 'Yes?' And you asked, 'Is George in?'

Ditto
The barmaid's only got little ones.

Ditto
The landlord threw you out, half an hour after drinking-up time. And threw the one-eyed gudgeon, with which you were making a spectacle of yourself, after you.

Ditto
When you announced, 'I'll fight any man who calls me a liar!', seven other people in the bar thumped you. It would have been eight if the battery on the last bloke's deaf aid hadn't run out.

The End-Of-The-Pier Show

Pier fishing offers real scope for the wallyangler. We're talking about a *real* pier, of course, with fortune tellers, one-armed bandits, go-karts, hall of mirrors, and a bar at the end; not one of your tatty little underdeveloped piers which are only good for landing boats at or fishing from.

The first essential is to pick a spot at the rail and spread yourself. Arrange your gear so that it takes up about ten feet of space on either side and stops anybody crowding you later on. (Not that you'll be there later on, but we'll come to that.)

Now for the cast. You can see all the amateurs casting out no more than thirty yards. That's not for you, poncing about like that. With your four-ounce lead you send the bait swishing out to sea. A hundred yards if it's an inch ... about seventy yards beyond where the fish are feeding.

But what the hell? You've achieved something with that cast. And you need to feel you've achieved something, because not all your casts get beyond the rail. One out of three picks up something on the backswing: a kiss-me-quick hat, a stick of candy floss, toffee apple, inflatable Snoopy Dog or – if you're really on form – a complete old lady.

Sometimes the backswing ends in a dull clunk, as the weight makes contact with the skull of a passing holidaymaker. Careless, that: they should look where they're going. Ought to know better than to walk behind you.

The contact may have been strong enough to have rendered the holidaymaker unconscious, which gives you time to pack up and move off before he comes round. If it has rendered him dead, which is more serious, you must sacrifice some of your valuable fishing time to console his sorrowing widow. Sentiments such as, 'Thank God it missed his eye', or, 'At least the fresh air did him good', are quite in order here.

Let's assume you've done nothing worse then hook an old lady or two and have finally cast out. The next move is to spread the surplus mackerel bait – guts, heads, tails and strips – on the boards behind you. This is so people can slip on them.

By the time people do slip on them, you're usually in the bar, but be ready should they come a cropper while you're still lashing your rod to the rail. To frail and elderly cropper-comers, you can deliver a stern lecture on the need for care when promenading on piers. And just look what a mess they've made of your bait. Fit for nothing now. Doesn't grow on trees, you know.

To large, fit and aggressive cropper-comers, shrug helplessly, give out with a few sympathetic *Tssk-tssks*, roll your eyes and incline your head in the direction of the bloke fishing next to you.

But all this is by the way. It's time for the really important part of your day on the pier. Lash the rod firmly to the rail, clip a bell to the tip, and make for the bar.

Firmly resolved not to allow any sloppiness to creep into your angling methods, you take your first pint to the bar window. From there you see if your rod-top dips, can just about hear the bell, and can enjoy the sight of the cropper-comers going base over candyfloss on your bait.

By the end of the pint, your eyes are beginning to feel the strain of staring at the rod, so you move further into the bar and get into conversation with other wally-anglers, telling yourself you'll hear the bell when it goes off. Discovering later that you can hear nothing but the roar of the sea and Wally Wurlitzer on his electronic organ, you decide to leave the bar and inspect the rod at the end of every pint.

On the first three or four inspections, nothing's happened at all. On the fifth – What's this? A complete stranger has untied your rod and is reeling it in with something big on the line. Cheeky sod! Hands off that rod, you swine! I've been watching it like a hawk all morning and as soon as I've got a bite – What? *And* you! Fancy your chances, eh...? My God, if I were six months younger...

*   *   *

By the time the bar closes, your interest in the prospects from the pier has widened, so you wander around to check the catches of others. Nice codling that bloke's got. Mind if I have a look? By heck, look at the size of that mouth. Amazing how the body tapers away so sharply, too. Could quite easily slip out of your – Whoops!

All right, all right. No need to be like that. Could happen to anybody. If he had a dropnet with him, he might be able to fish it back up again. If the tide wasn't taking it away so fast. Don't know what he's moaning at, anyway. Plenty of time to catch another if he's *that* clever.

Let's go and inspect that conger over there. Just look at those teeth! Feel the points on them! You wouldn't catch me doing this if the thing wasn't stone – Sheesh!

... Nice people in the First Aid room. Is that all they give you, though – a jab and a cup of tea? After a bite like that? What do you have to do to get a scotch – lose a leg? Still, let's get away from this rabble on the rails. Don't seem to be too popular for some reason.

Ah, there's the place. The jetty. Not a soul on it. What's that notice? DANGER: NO FISHING FROM THIS JETTY. Danger, my foot. Just a dodge by the locals to keep the place to themselves.

Right, here we are. Safely under the rope and down the steps. Danger! Huh! There's the spot, at the end. Just across those planks marked with yellow crosses. Wonder what they mean, those yellow crosses. Probably some sort of - Aaaaaarrrgh!

... This water's a lot colder than it looks. But not to worry; they've seen me. That's the Pier Master up there, calling words of encouragement. What's he shouting? Bloody what? Have a care, my good man: I'm a friend of the Chief Constable!

Now, what's the drill until the lifeboat arrives?

ONE: Don't panic.

TWO: Kick off gumboots. Who the hell thought that one up? Bet he never tried kicking off gumboots in a swell like this. Nothing for it but -

THREE: *Our Father, which art in ...*

Wallies Afloat

It's fun enough being a wallyangler on dry land, but it's nothing to the fun you can have afloat. Taking out a rowing boat doesn't just extend the range of your fishing, it extends your wallypotential no end.

Try not to go out alone. Two wallies always were better than one. And if you can get six in a boat meant for four, you're really in business.

As soon as you board the boat, you can start with a few old Goon Show lines:

'Cast off fore, aft and ift!'

'Aye-aye, Cap'n!'

See if you can manage to fall in the water. This gives you a chance for:

'Gad! That water was taller than me!'

And for your wallymate to reply: 'It's older, that's why, Neddy...'

As you pull away from the bank, it is essential for one of you to sit in the stern chanting, 'In...Out...In...Out...' and for the rest of you to burst into the Wallyboating Song:

> *Wally boating weather,*
> *Speeding through the breeze...*
> *Swing, swing together,*
> *Your rowlocks between your knees...*

Some boats are issued with paddles instead of oars, these being recommended as making for a quieter approach to

46

the fish. Quieter approach? What wally worth his salt wants a quieter approach? The paddles are ideal for the Wally of the River routine:

> Aye-ee-o-KO!
> Aye-ee-o-KO!
> Sandi the strong ...
> Sandi the wise ...

And as half a dozen Wallybosambos pull away from the shore, the boat owner is laughing heartily. He's never heard such jolly and original wit before. Just listen to his affectionate valediction: 'Pillocks! Hope you bloody drown...'

There's a fair chance of his parting wish coming true. It's very unwally, for a start, to board a boat sober. This could lead to everyone getting in in good order, stowing the gear evenly and arranging themselves properly around the boat. Which is very boring for everybody concerned.

It's very unwally, also, not to take on board the really essential supplies: half a dozen crates of ale, three or four bottles of scotch, and a couple of packets of sandwiches. What you're going to do with all that food is a bit of a problem, but it's usually resolved a few hours later by throwing the butties at each other.

Pay particular attention to your oarsmanship. Ideally, you ought to catch a crab at every third or fourth stroke, falling back into the boat and scooping the oars inboard so that everybody gets a good soaking. This allows your wallymates to retaliate by dipping a bait can into the water and pouring it down your neck.

Anchoring the boat gives plenty of scope. Many small boats have a large weight instead of the conventional anchor. You could pick this up from a sitting position and lower it gently over the side, but this doesn't add to the jollity. For real wallyfun, pick it up and stand in the bows. From here you have choices of routines:

1. Go straight over the side with it, bellyflopping for maximum splash.

2. Stand teetering in indecision. This allows a wallymate to join in the fun by putting his boot in your backside and giving a shove.

Yell loudly as you go overboard. This alerts other boaters, who may not be aware of the entertainment being offered.

In the absence of anything else to do, you may even get your tackle assembled and cast out. You've not bothered with short boat rods; not much fun potential in them. You all got 14- or 16-footers, which make for the maximum clashing of rod tips and tangling of lines.

Break the monotony by changing places every so often. Stand up to do this, and keep your rods in your hands. If one of you isn't overboard by the time you've done it twice, you're not really trying.

One way to get everyone changing places frantically is to stand in the bows and pee into the wind. Not only does this impart a sense of urgency, it adds immensely to the sophistication.

In the unlikely and unlucky event of anyone hooking a fish – which is not what wallyboating is all about – don't spoil the fun by having everybody else reel in and sit quietly. Everybody must jump and down, offering advice and splashing landing nets over the side. If all of you do this on the same side of the boat, you're almost certain to achieve the wallyevent you set out for – the whole lot of you pitching overboard. It is best to do this after all or most of the booze has been consumed. There's always a chance of the boat overturning and the precious cargo going to the bottom. Even for wallyfun, some prices are too high to pay.

You may as well pack up after that and make your way back. The fun isn't over, though, by a long way. You can veer close to other anchored boats and see how many lines you can cross or snarl up in the oars. Row around in circles shouting, 'Come in Number Seven – your time's up!' Shout sophisticated witticisms at any girls sunning themselves on other boats.

Choose from such classics as:

'Come over here, darlin' and feel my rowlocks!'

'I've got a longer one than he has!'

'Put some clothes on – you'll catch your death!'

'Could you tell your friend his wife's waiting for him?'

In the unlikely event of her replying, 'I *am* his wife,' reply – quick as a flash – 'That's not what *she* said. And he'd better hurry up – she's eight months gone!'

When you approach the landing stage, make the most of your last minutes afloat. If a lone, little and weedy angler is disembarking from another boat, ram it. If it's several large and fierce-looking anglers, ram the landing stage instead. If the boatyard owner isn't around, you've still time to fall in the water, lose an oar over the side, or pull the plug from the bottom of the boat and throw it away.

What a day, eh? Now you can make your way to the pub to dry off and get some serious drinking in.

A WALLY ALONE

But what of the lone wallyboater? How can he find his fun? Indeed, what point is there, with no wallymates to applaud him?

Have no fear, lone wallyboater. Do not despair. You can make your mark on the environment, impress your personality on the angling scene. And at the end of the day, which is the only wallyway of putting it, you can say proudly and without fear of contradiction, 'Alone I did it'.

Off you go, rowing or paddling a bit less flamboyantly than if you had company. Nobody to laff, what's the point? And wally actions are not made just for cheap and immediate acclaim. It may take longer, but if you can stick to your principles you can turn out as much a disaster as any bunch of show-offs.

You step into the boat with nobody to know or care whether you fall in or burst into song. Nobody to give a sod about whether you cast off first and step in second, leaving you with one leg in the boat and one leg on the bank, exposed to the risk of double hernia, double pneumonia, or both. Apart from the boatyard proprietor, that is, but he's seen it all before.

So you're on your own. And everything you do from now on is for your own satisfaction. Who the hell needs anybody else? Right, then. Off we go.

The sudden jerk and consequent whiplash effect happens because you forgot to untie the boat before you rowed off. See? Already you've made a start.

Before you've gone very far you'll catch a crab. Not at all intentionally, and for that very reason you'll forget to dip the oar inboard. Instead, you'll lose it. And spend the next half hour rowing frantically round in circles trying to retrieve it. You could have stuck the remaining oar over the stern and sculled in a more or less straight line, but that wouldn't have been wally at all.

You can always go over the side with the weight when you drop anchor, but in the absence of an audience, you do miss the thrill of the applause and the positive feedback of your mates hitting you over the head with a paddle as you try to climb back aboard. So just get on with it.

You're anchored now. It wasn't a complete waste of time, because you've anchored over the bow on a long rope. The boat is now swinging with the current in a graceful arc, finishing beyond casting distance of the spot you intended to fish.

Not to worry: this gives you the chance to cast upstream, so that your bait comes straight back towards you and travels under the boat. Makes for a lot of simulated bites, does that, as your float dips to follow the line. Makes for a lot of breaks, too, as you strike into a line that's tangled up somewhere beneath the stern. You'll have something to tell the wallylads back at the pub tonight: all those quick-biting monsters lying just under the boat.

Canal fishing seems harmless enough, but what you can do with a pair of manually-operated locks is nobody's business. Moor the boat and open the first lock. Feel the enormous sense of power as the water surges through. Leap back into the boat, move through first lock, then close it. Row to the second lock, and open it.

Watch the level go down as the water drains away with frightening rapidity. Watch the boat disappear, joining all the plastic cups, detergent foam, empty cans of wallybooze, in the rush of water through the gates. Either that or, as the water disappears, the boat is left high and dry, dangling from the towpath bollard with all the tackle falling out. Pity you didn't pay more attention to the procedure and recommended mooring knots, but who the hell's got time to learn all that stuff?

Perhaps you're better off away from the canal. Dead common, anyway, canals. Get yourself out on the river. Something of a challenge there. So down we go, keeping to the right. And there we are: a perfect fishing spot over on the left. A quick turn to port – or is it starboard? – and we're cutting right across the bows of an approaching vessel. Well, sod him, for a start. Steam gives way to sail, so diesel must give way to – Oops! Yes – and up yours as well, mate! Bloody capitalist!

... Perhaps your trip out has been uneventful. No wrecks and nobody drowned. Nothing to laff at at all.

You've done all the other wally things that guarantee a fishless day: stomped around the boat, sending out underwater vibrations that clear off the fish for yourself and everybody else within 200 yards; knocked out your pipe on the gunwales; knocked off the top of a bottle on the rowlocks. Perhaps in spite of that you've actually caught something – my God – it's a pike!

Now, don't panic. Or, if you do, panic properly. You've got the pike inboard and it's thrashing around, gnashing its teeth and making lunges at your vitals. What to do? Do the wally thing and try to stamp on it. Kick it to death. Or stay calm. And do the other wally thing: unsheath your wallybowie knife and lunge at its head. As the pike leaps over the side, as they tend to do in such situations, your wallybowie goes straight through the planks.

Nothing for it but to make your way back downriver. Easy enough. Just let the boat drift and you'll sort out all the probs.

First thing to do is to pull out the bowie knife, allowing a gush of water to enter the boat. You are reluctant to put back the knife, which cost a bob or two down at the wallytackle shop, so you try bailing with your bush hat. Not terribly successful, on account of its floppyness, but at least you tried. Only one thing for it now: pull out that plug in the bottom of the boat. Why didn't you think of that before? Let all the water out in no time.

What's that notice you're floating past? Boatyard thattaway. Fifty yards upstream. Damn! You've passed it. Better turn back and... but what's that other notice? DANGER! WEIR. Nobody said anything about a weir. What the hell's a weir doing on this stretch of – Oops!

You've made it, lad. Don't worry, you'll soon dry out. And the boat was bound to be insured. Just take comfort in the thought that you've done what you set out to do. And alone you did it...

And alone you did it . . .

With Baited Breath

It's not very wally to collect and prepare your own baits –
in moderation. To put the wallyness into it, you have to
work at it.

Take the common earthworm. You can usually get
enough of these by keeping a corner of the flowerbed
watered, laying a couple of old sacks on the top, or having
a quick sort through the compost heap. But the wallyway
is much more fun.

There are two wallyways, in fact. One is worm
charming. You stick a garden fork in the ground and
vibrate it, keeping a sharp eye open for worms which
surface to avoid the vibrations.

Sometimes it works, sometimes it doesn't. But either
way it provides an interesting spectator sport for the
neighbours as you stand there on the front lawn
twanging away in a passable imitation of Felix Men-
delssohn and His Hawaiian Serenaders (still much
beloved of elderly musical wallies), pausing only to
pounce whenever a worm emerges.

The second method is even wallier: stalking at night.
Wait for rain or a heavy dewfall, then creep out on to the
lawn in your stockinged feet, carrying a torch. (Stockinged feet are essential if you are not to alarm the worms
with a heavy footfall. Luckily, their sense of smell isn't up
to much.)

Switch on the torch and there are the worms, blinking
in the light. You have to move fast before they bolt back
into their holes. And you have to go for the tail which is

tucked into the hole, ready for a quick getaway.

Telling the difference between a worm's head and tail, especially by torchlight, is one of the wallyskills which comes only after long practice, so be prepared at first to finish up with only bits of worm. (If it's the head end, you're OK: it can still eat. The rear end has difficulty making the adjustment.)

You'll need a can, of course, to put the worms or the bits in. Carrying this as well as the torch can be cumbersome and slow down the action. So you take the wallyness a step further and do what Canadian professional worm-catchers do: tie a tin to each leg. As you kneel down to pick up each new worm, the worms in the tins tend to fall out, but at least you tried. Perhaps the Canadian worm-catchers are better at it.

To avoid the juggling with the torch, you can wear a miner's helmet with a flashlight built into the front; the perfect equipment for wallyworming. It does take a bit of explaining, though, when you're arrested in the middle of the night after a phone call to the police from suspicious neighbours.

'Stockinged feet? Miner's helmet? A tin tied to each leg? And catching worms, were we? At two in the morning? Sarge – we've got a right one 'ere...'

Oh, and next morning you tend to go down with a sneezing fit. Be prepared.

* * *

Pigeon droppings have an intermittent vogue among wallybait specialists, especially after the dastardly French, Belgians or Italians do well in international fishing matches. Mixed in the groundbait, the droppings are irresistible to fish. At least they are in the warmer waters of the Continent. In Britain they don't seem to make much difference. But that does not deter the wallybaiter.

There is a small snag, in that pigeon droppings are

never around when you want them. All the pigeons that for years have been dropping things on your head, suddenly disappear or drop things on somebody else. At this stage, local pigeon fanciers find themselves suddenly popular in the pub and besieged by offers of free mucking-out. But if you have no local pigeon fanciers, or your deadly rival has got in first, what do you do?

You could try haunting Trafalgar Square, wiping down bespattered tourists, or doing the same thing on seaside piers and hoping that seagull droppings will work just as well. Or ply pub parrots with crisps and sunflower seeds to the detriment of their health. Or even turn as a last resort to your own much-loved budgie. But beware: the RSPCA is concerned about the growing incidence of budgie abuse by wallyanglers, especially in single-budgie households. It would be little to your credit to be hauled before the magistrates on a charge of budgie-battering, even though your plea of insanity would come up against no opposition.

* * *

The collection of wasp grubs is a bit hazardous on account of the way the adult wasps get so peeved about it. But because of their excellence as bait, the grubs are worth the trifling inconvenience and hazard involved in their collection. With a bit of thought, you can wally-up the inconvenience and hazard into full-scale dangers to life and limb.

The first step is to locate a wasps' nest. They're often built underground or in eaves or lofts, and are not immediately visible to the naked eye. A true wallymethod, the subject of correspondence in *The Times*, is to catch a wasp, cover it with flour, and release it. It will fly in a straight line to the nest, the flour coating making it easy to follow.

Take warning, however, from the fate of one of the correspondents, who really did give chase the wallway: he followed the wasp down his garden at a swift run, whereupon his pursuit came to an abrupt and painful end. The wasp noticed the ten-foot wall at the bottom of the garden. He didn't.

There are three common wallymethods of collecting the wasp grubs:

1. Using a beehive smoke-puffer to quieten the wasps. It works on bees, but if there's anything a wasp can't stand, it's having smoke puffed all over it. Just you wait until it's stopped coughing...

2. Using a proprietary agricultural wasp-killer, placed in the entrance to the nest, and then covered over to let the poison gas do its worst. The poison, which is arsenic-based, is very effective: not just at killing wasps, but also at killing the wallies who stand around the nest waiting for it to work.

3. Using an aerosol whose label proclaims that it kills all flying insects stone dead. As you are running for cover or diving into the water butt, you've the consolation of knowing that at least you've confirmed the long-held theory that wasps can't read.

If the truth were told, there's only one safe and painless method of collecting wasp grubs; let your mate do it.

*   *   *

Elderberries in season (and when else can you get 'em?) make a useful and plentiful bait. Half an hour in a good elder hedge can produce several large bucketsful of elderberries, which you can leave in the kitchen over-night. Earwigs, too, are handy things to have, and by morning you'll have plenty; elderberry clusters being favourite venues for mass earwig rallies. All you have to do is to collect them from the kitchen walls, out of the pantry, from under the sink and out of the chip pan. Comb carefully through the cat to pick up any stragglers.

*   *   *

Maggots are the universal all-purpose bait, and their breeding is ridiculously simple. The true back-to-basics wally can use the original method – hanging a dead sheep over a tubful of bran – though this can lead to problems if you live in a high-rise flat.

You may have to settle for the more conventional method: laying a piece of meat in a bucket of bran or sawdust, on which bluebottles can lay their eggs. Nor need it be just any old meat: to attract different kinds of flies, which produce different kinds of maggot, you can use liver, pig's heart, pigeons or fish. Within a week, the flesh, fish or fowl will be heaving with maggots and smelling like a mass grave of lucky socks.

While all this this going on, you might like to prepare some baits in the kitchen. Hemp is a favourite, stewed in the wife's non-stick pan, to which it sticks very well and gives off a revolting smell while so doing. Still on the back-to-basics kick, you can heat up some greaves – a mixture of tallow waste, from which you pick out the best bits of fat – and bullocks' pith. Bullocks' pith, you thimply chop into pietheth.

Stick some breadcrusts in the oven to bake for your groundbait. They're done when the canary falls off its perch; overdone when the cat is laid low by the choking black smoke.

And there you are – ready for anything with worms, pigeon droppings, wasp grubs, elderberries, earwigs, maggots, stewed hemp, greaves, bullocks' pith, and charcoal-flavoured groundbait.

'But what of my wife?' you may ask. What will she think of all this? Will she have no complaints about the requisitioning of her kitchen and the revolting mixture of foul smells wafting in and around the house?

Don't worry. There'll be no complaints. In fact you won't hear so much as a word from the lady. She'll have left you weeks ago.

Wallying On

By now you will have learned enough elementary skills to pass muster as a basic wallyangler. And perhaps you feel the urge to move on, to specialise a bit, to fine down your areas of activity and impress your developing personality more firmly on the angling scene.

Here follow some specialised approaches to the art, each guaranteed to get you noticed. Not loved, perhaps, but certainly noticed.

EVERYTHING BUT...

Angling is full of surprises, and no two days are alike. So be prepared to Be Prepared. Follow the example of the Kitchen Sinker, often an Eager Beaver in a previous incarnation.

He finishes work early on Fridays, if he goes at all. He has to: it takes until the small hours of Saturday morning to get everything ready. (His lady wife, meanwhile, retires early to bed. Often with a Mills & Boon novel, box of chocolates and bottle of gin. She knows better than to get in the way.)

He starts with the bait. Breadpaste, cheesepaste, flake, crust. Sliced loaf for punched bread. Several cans of maggots: gozzers, pinkies, specials, squatts, anattos. And a big tin of casters.

Worms from the scouring tins: lobworms, brandlings, redworms and blueheads. If his eyesight's up to it, some bloodworms from the water butt.

A quick clean-out of the pantry for sweetcorn, luncheon meat, frankfurters, peas. Get the pans simmering with wheat, hemp, pearl barley, macaroni, rice and spuds. A safari round the garden while the light lasts for slugs and snails, earwigs and caterpillars, perhaps a near-suicidal raid on a wasps' nest. While the swellings are going down, time to mix up several different consistencies of ground-bait, each with its own Secret Ingredient.

That'll have to do to be going on with. Perhaps pick up some elderbrerries and swan mussels at the water. Time to organise the tackle:

Match rods, ledger rods, river rods, roach poles, fly rod. And boat rod just in case. Three king-sized keepnets and carp-sized landing net.

Check the cabinet of floats: Avons, antennae, sticks, balsas, balsa-and-sticks, crows, porcupines, peacocks, zoomers, wagglers, sliders and bubbles.

Check the cabinet of lines, weights, hooks, swim-feeders, blockends, disgorgers, forceps, spring balances, thermometers. Case of spoons, spinners, flies, plugs. Reels ... fixed spools, closed face, centrepins, multipliers.

Baskets, bait waiters, bank sticks, rod rests, catapults, brolly, tent, windbreaks, groundbait bucket, tackle trolley, picnic hamper, stove, spirit lamp, handwarmer, foot muff and nose cosy.

Now we're getting somewhere. Spare pullovers, parkas ...

The car is loaded with the basics in the early hours, an operation not looked upon with much favour by neighbours who open their bedroom windows and shout abuse or throw things. After a couple of hours' sleep, our hero is up and at it again, braving further neighbourly hostility, which may include a visit from the bleary-eyed Incredible Hulk next door, who jumps on his gozzers and hits him with the cat.

But, with luck, he's off; boot, back seat and roof rack packed solid.

At the venue, he has a problem: whether to carry all his

Time for that magic first cast...

gear to the water in stages or to attempt it one go. Both have their drawbacks. Doing it in stages means that a lot of the gear he left on the bank on the first trip is no longer around when he arrives on the second, the Brotherhood of the Angle being what it is. Carrying it in one go gives him a funny walk and makes his eyes water; early warnings of an incipient double hernia.

Eventually, he makes it, and spends a happy hour or two setting out his stall. There are a few holdups caused by other anglers who are not in sympathy with the thoroughness of his preparations. In the attempt to get to their own swims, they stumble into his gear, do themselves a mischief climbing over it, or kick it in the water.

Finally, he's ready. Snug in his windbreak under the brolly; tent set up behind in case the weather turns inclement. Water temperature taken, depths recorded, currents noted. Landing net set up, swim groundbaited and rod assembled. Time for that magic first cast.

It's a pity he can't see his float, darkness having fallen so quickly due to the unforeseen rotation of the Earth. Time to pack up. Good job he remembered the spirit lamp.

ON THE CADGE

The wallycadger is an example to us all in self-sufficiency. Not for him the vast outlay on tackle or bait. He travels light: rod, landing net and empty bait tin being his only encumbrances, and thumbs a lift to the water.

He takes his time finding a swim. He has a few calls to make first.

The smaller or less confident wallycadger taps up his fellow piscators one at a time, giving the impression of an amiable but forgetful or accident-prone angler whose day this is not.

'Hello there! Morning, morning. Grand day, isn't it? By heck, I was so looking forward to it. But you know what

I've gone and done? Left my maggots at home. Forget my head if it was loose. Well, I suppose there's nothing for it but to trail all the way back. Miss the best part of the day. Still, it's my own fault. Nobody to blame but...'

With luck, his fellow angler will take pity on him and offer a double handful of maggots. 'Most kind. Really. Er... You haven't got a plastic bag I could put them in...?' (No sense in wasting the bait tin at first cadge.)

Without luck, his fellow angler will not take the hint. Stage Two coming up:

'I hate to ask this, really I do. But you couldn't *sell* me half a dozen or so maggots, could you? My only day off this week. Shame to waste it. Especially after what the doctor told me...'

Sell is the buzzword. No experienced wallycadger says *give*. But he's seldom taken up on the offer to pay. If he is, a sudden cashflow problem sets in:

'Oh. Ah. Er. Silly me. I've done it again. Gave my wife all my spare cash last night to pay the vet's bills on our poor spaniel. Not long for this world, poor old thing. The spaniel, that is. Not that the wife's feeling too clever. Clean forgot to call at the cash dispenser this morning. You don't take Access, do you? Barclaycard? American Express?'

By now he's done it. And off he goes, after showering gratitude and blessings in profusion, to the next angler:

'Do you know what I've gone and done? Left my hooks at home. Brand new, they were, too. Only bought them yesterday. You wouldn't have a couple...?'

Within half an hour he's kitted out better than his less forgetful confrères and can settle down to a day's expense-free fishing.

The more confident wallycadger can collect several items in one visit – maggots, hooks, half a dozen shot, the odd float – gauging the moment when impatience is setting in, and ceasing to cadge at the first sign of it. Don't want to upset the punters, John.

But the seventeen-stone wallycadger has no trouble at

'You couldn't see your way clear...?'

all. He can get everything he wants just by flashing an empty bait tin and announcing, 'Morning. I've left the bloody lot at home today. Got me in a real strop, it has. I can only put it down to getting that summons for Grievous Bodily Harm this morning. Now you couldn't see your way clear...'

* * *

Brass-necked as he appears, however, the wallycadger is deeply sensible of the potential inconvenience imposed on a fellow angler by relieving him of his bait or tackle. What if the cadgee runs out of hooks or bait later in the day, both of which he would still have but for his misplaced generosity? What if he approaches the wallycadger and asks, ever so nicely, if he can have some of his stuff back?

Our wallycadger, mindful of what his fellow angler has done for him, and in full knowledge of the difference a small act of kindness can make, answers without the slightest hesitation.

'No, you can't,' he says. 'Bugger off.'

THE MAD MATCHMAN

OK, so you're a dedicated matchman. What's wrong with that? Nothing at all, until you wally it up a bit by letting the dedication get the better of you.

The Appliance of Science. That's the thing. None of your chuck-it-and-chance-it methods. No waffling on about the beauty of the waterside, the shimmering colours of a freshly caught fish, no sunlight filtering through the leaves, kingfishers flashing from bough to bough, that kind of rubbish. Above all, no laughing. This is serious, this is.

And there's nothing wrong with you. It's THEM. All those blokes out there, bent on doing you down. Attempting to steal the formula of your Secret Superbait.

Intent on nobbling you the night before the match by plying you with the Demon Drink, perhaps slipping you a Mickey Finn.

Nor do they give up on the bank: they're still at it. Fixing the draw so that you get the worst peg on the stretch. Trying to distract you by coughing – even more subtly, by breathing – as you sit intent on the next bite. Slipping noxious but undetectable substances into your swim. Playing in their own fish wide so that the splashing scares off the fish in front of your peg.

After all the preparation, too; all the time and trouble you took to ensure that you'd come out top on the big day. The Secret Superbait even further enriched by additives known only to yourself, flavours never known to fail on this particular stretch. Glueing those dust shot on the backsides of 750 casters, to make sure they'd each sink like a stone. The hours of practice on the lawn to ensure minimum time loss on the cast and reel-in.

All that time, as well, you spent on physical and mental preparation. The vitamin-enriched health food diet, jogging and yoga exercises, to make sure you were at the peak of your physical condition. The expensive specs you were fitted for to make sure you missed not the slightest tremble of the float. All that Nietzsche you read to get yourself mentally prepared. You were the greatest, you were Superman – *Ubermensch* – you were unbeatable. You couldn't have lost. It was impossible. Unthinkable. So how come you did?

Somebody's finger was under that scale basket when you weighed your fish in; they should have registered at least half a pound more than that. And what happened when you protested and demanded a re-weigh? Still the same weight. Those scales were rigged. It's a plot, you see. Those stewards are in league with the match secretaries of both teams. In the pay of the bookies, too, you shouldn't wonder.

Go and have a pint and forget it. There's always another time. But who are those blokes in the pub? It's

THEM. Hear what he said to you – 'Good afternoon'? What the hell did he mean by that? He's up to something, all right. And look what he's doing at the bar. Talking to those other blokes. And laughing!

Pound to a penny they're talking about you behind your back. In front of your face. Gloating over your humiliation. No doubt plotting how they're going to fix you next time. You've never seen those blokes before? Of course not. Just goes to show: even complete strangers are conspiring to do you down.

What's that he's asking you – 'What are you having?' First it's 'Good afternoon', now he's trying to ply you with drink. Must be trying to ingratiate himself; a bit late for a Mickey Finn now the match is over.

No, you're not stopping here to have all your secrets wormed out of you, free drinks or no free drinks. Get back home, that's the thing. Know you're safe there.

Ah, here's the wife. What's she saying? 'Hello, darling. How did it go?'

How did it go? She can tell from your face how it went. So *she's* after classified information too. Wonder how they got to her? Always thought she was over-friendly with that milkman.

Get upstairs and have a stiff scotch and a lie-down. That'll settle your mind a bit. What's this on the stairs? The cat, sniffing at your right welly. No doubt attracted by the latest additive to the Secret Superbait. Thought only dogs were attracted to anis – Hell! Nearly gave it away! Right, then, Tiddles – *you* can bugger off for a start... God, it comes to something when they've even subverted your faithful moggy.

Feeling better now? Nothing like booting the cat up the hallway to get things out of your system. Now then, next week's match. What do you reckon – maggies or casters...?

Just as there's a Life and Soul at every party, there's one in every angling pub. It's not one of the easiest wallycharacters to achieve and not recommended to anyone without a cheerful disposition, total dedication, unending flow of words and a high quality, steel-tempered, brass neck. No use even attempting it if you're sensitive enough to be put off by requests to sit down, shut up, sod off or drop dead.

If *The Compleat Angler* is anything to go by, Izaak Walton himself was a pioneer of the technique: button-holing compleat strangers and subjecting them to long, philosophical and sickeningly cheerful ear-bashings. The book's very first chapter starts with Walton, in his role as Piscator, catching up with a hunter and a falconer:

'You are well overtaken, Gentlemen! A good morning to you both! I have stretched my legs up Tottenham Hill to overtake you, hoping your businss may occasion you towards Ware, whither I am going this fine fresh May morning.'

Both hunter and falconer professed pleasure at meeting the old buffer – they couldn't do much else as he was writing the script – but after what they had to listen to before the end of the chapter, it's surprising that they ever let him overtake them again. ('Omygawd... It's bloody Walton again. Boring old fart. Too late – he's seen us...')

Things haven't changed much. Izaak Walton lives. Or at least his spiritual descendant does; Wally Walton, known to everyone in the pub as Mister Blah-Blah, Babbling Brook, or Pain-in-the-Bum.

It's easy enough to mock, but Wally Walton does have a purpose in life: to cheer everybody up, whether they like it or not; to impart priceless pearls of angling wisdom; and finally, to help them nod off into a well-earned rest with a remorseless flow of wallyspeak.

Into the pub he walks, wearing a hat covered with spinners that would frighten the life out of any known fish, a windcheater plastered with enough badges to bring a Rover Scout to his knees, and carrying enough gear to sink the *Titanic*.

The warning is hissed around the bar, 'Hey up – it's here!'

Potential victims scramble through the door into the next bar or dive under the tables. Those who can't, or who fall down in the attempt, sit mesmerised, awaiting their fate, like rabbits in front of a stoat.

It has been raining buckets and blowing a gale all morning. The anglers in the pub raised not a fish from the storm-lashed water. Half an hour ago they staggered in frozen stiff, soaked to the skin and thoroughly miserable, craving nothing but warmth, comfort, and a few pints of anaesthetic. Wally's going to change all that.

In he stomps, cheerful and beaming.

'Hello, gang!' he cries. 'Long time no see! I'll be with you in a minute. Half of cooking, landlord, if you'd be so kind...'

While his back is turned, there's another scramble for the door. But in the short time available, and with all the kicking and gouging going on, the smaller, slower or gentler souls are left to their fate.

Potential victims keep their eyes fixed firmly on the bottom of their pint pots. If they can't see him, perhaps he can't see them.

Walton knows everybody. 'Morning, squire! Lovely weather for ducks, what? Morning, you old rascal – still beating the wife? Har har. Sorry, madam – that was my carbon fibre that just took you amidships. Bet that tickled your fancy, eh?'

Those marked down for cheering up – eyes still tightly closed or with paper bags over their heads – hope he'll stop en route and afflict himself on one of his many other acquaintances, all of whom are intently studying their feet or the ceiling. But no. A promise is a promise. The heavy tread approaches remorselessly.

'Well, here I am, chaps! Finally made it. It's an ill wind,

eh? Thought I'd join you fair weather fishermen. Cheer you up a bit.'

He starts the cheering-up process with a game of musical chairs.

'Could I just dump my gear behind your seat, old boy? Sorry there's so much of it, but you never know what the day holds in store. Be prepared, that's my motto. As the cubmistress said to the bishop, what? Ha ha.

'Nearly there, old son. If I can just stick this rod – Oops! Terribly sorry, squire: I seem to have knocked your glass over. No good crying over spilt beer, eh? Good job it wasn't full. Not the best place to leave it, though, if I may make so bold.

'That's everything stowed away shipshape and Bristol fashion. Now then, room for a little 'un? If you'd just move up one, old son, I can sit on your seat. One man, one vote; one bum, one seat, I always say.

'Ah, that's better. Just pass the ashtray, will you, squire? Not too draughty over there, is it? Probably better for you than the heat from this fire.

'Right, you miserable lot! You gave up early, I must say. Spot of weather never hurt anyone. Give an account of yourselves!'

'Well, we –'

'Too easy, these days. To much mollycoddling. Country's going soft. Why, when I …' (Time passes, to the steady rhythm of *blah-blah-blah*.) 'So I said to him, I said, – Oh, if you're going to the bar, old chap. I'll have a large brandy. Look after the inner man, eh? "Call that a fish?" I said. 'I've fed bigger than that to our cat …'''

By now, four of the six victims have their eyes tightly closed, a phenomenon which he takes as a sign of concentration on his gripping monologue. He ignores the fifth one hanging from a low beam.

Yes, you shouldn't have left the bank so early, you lot. Just after you'd gone I was into this enormous pike.* Fought like a tiger.** Had me up and down the bank like a

---

*Wallyspeak for 1½ lb.
**Ditto for felt a little more virile than a wet lettuce.

fiddler's elbow. But the old magic's still there: I had him in the end. Well, I say *him*. Could have been a her. Yes, I couldn't tell whether it was an esox or a shesox. That's a good 'un – esox or shesox... Get it? Come on, lads – pull your sox up! *Sox* – with an X... Get it?

The last victim nods off, stunned finally into insensibility. It dawns on Wally that there's nobody left to buy him a drink, and that the conversation may have been a bit one-sided. So he tries to make amends, prodding the comatose form beside him.

'Anyway, that's enough about me. Let's talk about you. What do you think of my new carbon fibre job? Neat, eh? Got it discount, of course. Only cost me...'

JEEPERS WEEPERS

To be fair, a dose of Wally Walton can be a help to somebody who's down in the dumps, if only to make him realise that things could be worse, and to motivate him enough to make a run for the other bar. But Wally has no effect at all on Jeepers Weepers. Jeepers is beyond all hope. Hardly anything ever goes right for him.

If something nice does happen, he may cheer up enough to stop snivelling for a while. But something else always happens to spoil it. When he catches a potential record fish for the stretch, he's actually smiling as he plonks it down in the pub for the admiration of the throng. But while his back's turned, the landlord's dog snatches the fish off the table and pulls it to pieces in the yard.

'Is this a wally worth emulating?' you may well ask. What percentage is there in being miserable all the time? But consider. If it's not you who are wrong, but the world; if your best laid plans gang aft agley; if you generally end the day wishing you'd never got out of bed, you may as well give into it and have a damn good wallywallow in self-pity. Gets it out of your system. And if it doesn't, it's usually good for a few free pints from luckier anglers who try to cheer you up.

Even Wally Walton has no effect on Jeepers Weepers

A typical Jeepers is the lad who staggers into the pub soaking wet, his rod tip smashed beyond repair, with not a fish to show for it.

'You've been in the wars,' says the landlord. 'What's happened?'

'Had a row with the bailiff,' says Jeepers. 'Told him where to stuff his tickets. He wrapped the rod round my neck and threw me in the water.'

'Tough,' says the landlord.

'That's not all,' continues Jeepers. 'A month ago my wife left me. A couple of weeks ago I lost my job. The HP company repossessed the car and the telly. The building society foreclosed on my mortgage. Then the house burned to the ground. It wasn't insured, either.'

'You're not having the luck, are you?'

'Oh, I don't know,' says Jeepers. 'I'm not taking things lying down. I've started up in business on my own.'

'Good for you. What are you doing?'

'Selling lucky white heather on the bank.'

... Jeepers' tales of woe are some consolation to other anglers who realise that their day's run of bad luck is nothing by comparison. And as he catalogues his misfortunes – got up late, car broke down, maggots chrysalised in the heat, lost two sets of terminal tackle in the trees, outfall from the bleach factory got into his swim, eaten alive by gnats, ducks pinched his groundbait, wash from boat set his keepnet adrift, fell in the water – he gets a lot of sympathy and free pints.

But neither sympathy nor free pints lift him from his depression. In fact it gets worse as the evening wears on. He's the last in the pub, sunk into a catatonic trance of self-pity. And as the landlord frogmarches him towards the door, he points to the huge pike in the glass case and yells, 'The bloke who caught that fish is a bloody liar!'

It's highly wally to be the first one to cast out at the opening of the Coarse Season. To arrive at the water several hours before midnight on June 15 to be sure of getting a good spot, and to wait, along with dozens of other like-minded wallyanglers, for the stroke of twelve.

During the waiting time you give your views to three reporters: one from the local paper, the second from *Insomniacs' Hour* on the local radio station, the third a genuine Fleet Street stringer who was under the mistaken impression there'd be free booze laid on.

'Yerss ... I reckon I'll be first in, all right. Three months I've been practising for this, and I reckon my reflexes are on peak form. It's all in the wrist, you see ...

'Won't be long before you see results, either. There are bigger fish in here than ever came out, and I'm going to be into one of 'em.'

As midnight strikes, out goes your line in the superb long-distance wallycast you've been practising since the end of last season. And you're into something straight away! What is it? Tench? Carp? Catfish? By the power of its pull it's certainly a –

'Moo ...'

Not to worry. If you actually hit the water it would take some of the wallyness out of things. If you caught a fish, it would take all of the wallyness out of things.

You're better sticking to the long-distance casting and the true wallycatches: cows, sheep, trees, brick walls, gasometers, courting couples, juggernauts, all-night buses, high-voltage overhead cables, and the London-to-Glasgow express.

Country Life

Nothing like a day's fishing in the country. Get away from all the smoke, muck and noise of the town. Into God's good air. But you must do it properly if you're to gain the full wallybenefit.

You need some distinctive transport for a start. Range Rover, Land Rover (both completely different from a hedgehog*) are fine. Even wallier are Japanese or American runabouts which look like an upmarket jeep or souped-up builder's truck, with names such as Shogun, Samurai, Maverick, Laredo, Mohawk, Cherokee, etc. The original trim is usually very butch, but you can improve on it by having it painted in full camouflage or with safari-park zebra stripes.

Mount a piece of plastic drainpipe on the top. This not only holds the rods, but makes it look as if you're about to zap a tank at any second.

The advantage of such transport lies not only in its looks. When you arrive at the spot you can drive across pasture and ploughland, sown land, mown land, downland and upland, to get to the water. Leave the gates open behind you: saves a lot of time on the way back. The open gates also give you, on looking back or doing a U-turn, the full effect of the tracery made by your four-wheel drive over the different surfaces of the fields. Such interesting

---

*If you don't know why, ask someone. The answer is not something we'd care to include in a high-class instruction manual such as this.

textures. And it might encourage you to try a few figure-eights on the more friable surfaces.

While you're at it, why not try rounding up the odd herd of bullocks, aided by nothing but the souped-up horsepower under the bonnet? Surprising how fast they can run when they put their minds to it..

Here we are, at the water. Let's get cast out, then, and open a few cans. Ah, that's better. Nothing like fresh air for giving you a thirst. Save the empty cans. And the bottles. When things get quiet you can sling them in the water or range them along the top of a wall and get in some target practice with your .22 or air rifle.

Let's have the old cassettes on while you're waiting for a bite. An earful of Frankie Laine. Makes you feel you're right out there in the wide open spaces. Turn it up a bit. Spot of Tex Ritter, Slim Whitman as well. What a life those boys have, eh? Riding the range. Rounding up the dogies. Punching the old cows.

Talking of which – those bullocks have come back through the gate from the next field. Never learn, do they? Let's give them a run for it. Hee-yah! Woah – hee! Round 'em up, head 'em out, Rawhide ...!

By heck, they didn't stay long. Never mind: we've got those sheep over there. Get your wellies on, lads! Maa-aaaah! Gerrup there!

Phew ... Takes it out of you. Still not a twitch on the rods. Let's get some grub down us. Big fry-up. Nothing like it, over an open fire. Get one going under those trees, out of the wind. And let's have some stones off the top of that dry stone wall to hold it in. Don't want to set the undergrowth alight. Country Code and all that.

Sausages, bacon, eggs, tinned tomatoes, fried bread. Can't whack it. Just chuck the wrappings under that hedge. Soon get grown over. Sling a bit more wood on the fire: keep the midges off.

While it's quiet, let's stack some stones from that wall into the back of the van. Look smashing in that rockery back home.

No luck with the rods yet? What kind of water is this? Anbody fancy climbing a tree? Tell you what, race you to the top. Me Tarzan. Aah-ah*ah*-ah-*ah*-aaaaaaaah!

Phwarh! That was fun. Can't trust those branches, though. It was touch-and-go when that big one broke.

Right... let's look at those rods. Looks like a nibble on – Hey up! Who's this? Looks like some sort of a farmer. None too pleased, at that. And what's that he's raising to his shoulder? Looks like a – Eek!

*   *   *

Tell you what, you're not going to take this lying down. Having to leave all the gear at the water like that. Only just escaping with your life. There'll be a strong complaint on the club secretary's desk on Monday morning. My God, if you can't enjoy a quiet day's fishing in the country without some loony peppering the seat of your pants...

Some Side-Splitting Wallyjapes: 2

Wallyanglers are often in possession of dead fish, it being not in their nature to return decent-sized specimens to the water. But once you've got them, what do you do with them?

Taking fish home for the cat is very wally. The preparation of the fish is simple enough: you just leave it in the fridge, or lying around the kitchen, for a couple of weeks until the clutter or the smell brings complaints from your Nearest and Dearest. Then you either wrap the fish tightly in a plastic bag and bung it at the bottom of the dustbin, or take it down the garden and bury it deep in the veg plot.

Statistics show that of every 100 fish taken home for the cat, only 0.5 per cent ever see the inside of the moggy. And of this 0.5 per cent, only half is actually cooked. The other half is stolen by the cat, eaten raw, and thrown up within minutes.

What if you do brave the pong and mess to clean the fish, cook it and serve it up? It's a mighty cat that can see off a 25 lb tope or 12 lb pike in a few sittings. Soon it's fleeing the house to escape its fifteenth helping of shark meat since Tuesday, and pining for the good old days of Chicken Flavoured Jellymeet Gee-Gee Chunks.

So there you are, embarrassed by a profusion of dead fish. You could have put them put back alive in the water, but that would have left you with no evidence of your incredible skill as a wallyangler. (You could have put them back dead in the water, but that would have made the whole thing seem rather pointless, wouldn't it? Even wallies have feelings.)

What to do? Use them for side-splitting wallyangler fishjapes, that's what to do.

The most common use for dead pike, for instance, is to leave one stuffed down the back of the settee at your mate's house after a post-piscatorial philosophy session. His wife is so incensed on her return from shopping to discover a comatose husband surrounded by empty cans, overflowing ashtrays and smouldering carpets, that her instincts fail her: she neglects to look for the dead fish that is the calling card of every true wallyangler.

After spending a week disinfecting every room in the house, pouring bleach down the drains, ripping up floorboards and calling in the sanitary man, she finally discovers the decomposing pike. She is not well pleased.

A refinement of the dead-pike jape, with quicker results, is to sneak upstairs at your mate's house and deposit the pike in the marital couch. If you can ascertain which is the wife's side, it adds immeasurably to the fun. Stick the fish far enough down under the covers so that she feels it before she sees it. There's nothing like a cold fish on a warm bum to set the night resounding to screams of affronted femininity, especially if the pike has its mouth open at the time.

The bigger the fish, the better. And the uglier. Pike, shark and catfish have seldom ranked high in the lists of piscatorial pulchritude; especially the catfish, which makes Quasimodo look like Boy George.

You can dispose of defunct sharks quite soon after landing, and preferably at night, by tying them to lamp posts, propping them up in telephone kiosks with the receivers stuck under their gills, leaving them with their heads sticking out of drain covers, or dumping them in the municipal swimming pool.

But walliest of all is to leave them in a pub loo. Not just leave them, but tastefully to arrange them for maximum shock effect. It works well enough in the Gents, especially towards closing time, but to spread real terror, it's best applied in the Ladies.

You have to pick a quiet time, be quick about it, and leave a like-natured, i.e. wallybund, mate on guard outside. Hang the shark on the back of the closet door. With any luck, the next occupant will not see it until she's sat down. She is then faced with a split-second decision: whether to pull up her knickers and run, or just run.

But for real rib-tickling, or bum-tickling, fun, shove a pike or catfish tail-first into the loo bowl with its head level with the seat, and close the lid. Again, with any luck, the presence will not be discovered until the next occupant has actually settled down. There's nothing like the dead-hand tickling of catfish whiskers on an unprotected maidenly botty to help a girl go up in the world.

* * *

Several large fish on a sea trip give enormous scope for wallypranks on the jetty, especially where several wallies are gathered together. Conger are the best. With half a dozen of these you can troop off the boat in single file, each with the head and tail of a conger clamped under an armpit, so that it looks as if you're carrying a thirty-foot eel.

Dance down the gangplank to the appropriate wallywit chant of 'Aye-Aye, Conger! Aye-Aye Conger!', to make sure that those gathered on the quayside are made aware of the happening, and then line up for a wide-angle-lens photograph with which you can amaze, mystify and bore the pants off those back home.

The overall effect can be spoilt if one of the congers wakes up, perhaps aroused and irritated by a ripe underarm odour which has been reinforced by a spraying of *Armpit Authority – The Mark of a Man*, and takes a chunk out of its bearer. But even this can be turned to advantage if the event is being recorded by a cine or video camera. You can have hours of jolly fun re-running the event at home or at club socials and slowing down the action at the crucial moment. Your afflicted fellow wally will probably enjoy it himself, as soon as he gets out of hospital.

With the smaller congers or larger freshwater eels, you can play the Big One joke. Stand in the Gents holding an eel where your own modest appendage should be, and wait for the admiring comments or gasps of envy and disbelief.

You can add verisimilitude to the routine by dashing into the Gents, eel akimbo, and panting, 'Phew! I've just made it!' Be prepared to have your thunder stolen by racist and eelist wallycracks such as, 'Can you make me one like that – only in white?'

Wallying In The Balance

Because of the money involved in prizes, side bets and sponsorship, match fishing inevitably attracts its share of cheats. Some of the tricks they get up to in an attempt to come away with first prize, you'd never believe. But sophisticated and devilish cunning tricks are not for the wally. What he uses are the tricks that are bound to be found out.

The commonest wallytrick is stuffing lead shot or spiral weights down a fish's gullet. This calls for the use of a dead fish, unless you are prepared to risk the thing throwing the lot up into the scale basket at the weigh-in. And dead fish usually attract a bit more attention, especially if they're half a pound over the weight-for-length scale or drop on a steward's foot and break his toe.

You can make a weighted fish look more passable by plumping it up, by inserting a straw in its vent and blowing. But you have to take the risk of its deflating before the weigh-in, or taking off from the scales going, 'Prrrrrrrrrppppp...' There's always the danger, too, of a flatulent fish blowing first, in which case you may not make the weigh-in, being too busy rushing around the bank and screaming for a stomach pump.

You can take your own fish to the water, stuffed down your wellies or in the poacher's pocket of your jacket, and pretend to catch them. These fish are often called into question on account of their being obviously long-dead. Sometimes, when used by a Grade A wally, it's on account of their being mackerel or dogfish; uncommon catches on the Grand Union Canal.

A common trick at the weigh-in is to take advantage of the pushing and shoving to slip the same fish through the basket twice. This is dodgy enough at the best of times, but as a dedicated wally you do it with the one-eyed fish with a couple of fins and half a tail missing, and perhaps a Water Authority metal tag clamped upon its person.

On the bank itself you can reduce the chances of the bloke next to you by accidentally throwing into his swim some groundbait which has been laced accidentally with soap powder. Unless he, too, is a wally matchman, he becomes aware of the foaming under his rod tip and remonstrates by reporting you to a steward or shoving a rod rest up your nose.

No use complaining. If it's only your nose, you've got off lightly.

The Upper Echelon

A recurring dream of every wallyangler is of being an upper crust game fisherman. Striding through the heather in pursuit of a cunning prey; hearing the scream of the reel as a monster salmon strips the line; relaxing in the evening with a glass of malt whisky by a peat fire. All that stuff.

But it has to be remembered that genuine upper crust game fishermen rate as Superwallies. They come from a long line of wallies stretching back to the Norman Conquest, or at least since Great-Grandpapa promised not to tell what he saw Queen Victoria and John Brown up to in the heather, and so was elevated to the peerage.

To become a fully fledged superwally is beyond the reach of most of us. It takes time, inbreeding and a lot of money. Eton, Sandhurst, the Guards; that sort of thing.

Such superwallies fish rivers where each salmon costs several thousand pounds to land. They do not have to worry too much about piscatorial skills, there being ghilliewallies to point out the fish, instruct on the cast, direct the playing and finally gaff or tail the fish. An upper crust superwally can bag several fish in a day and not have a trace of scale or slime on his person, having never actually handled the beastly things.

It is possible, however, to become an imitation upper crust gamefisher, which is one notch up from plain wally. It helps to have a receding chin, protruding teeth, outsize hooter and a laugh like a ruptured mule. The laugh comes easily with practice. If you don't have the other attributes, you'll just have to get along as best you can, unless you're well-britched enough to afford plastic surgery and a private dentist.

Stop reading the *Sun* or the *Mirror* and subscribe to *The Times* or *Telegraph* instead (the *Express*, at the very least, if the big words bother you). Give up the wallypleasures of *Playboy* and *Men Only* and concentrate instead on *The Field, Horse and Hound, Country Life*, and the various upmarket wallyangling magazines which cater for game fishers only.

Dress like an advert for twelve-year-old scotch, which you can do on an instant credit account at all good gents' outfitters. Tweed shooting jacket, plus-fours, brogues and a tweed hat which you decorate with flies. Don't worry about them falling out: once a fly's been stuck beyond the barb into a tweed hat, it's impossible to shift. Flies in hats are not for *fishing* with, dammit.

Then you'll need a game bag or wicker creel, a shorthandled landing net and, if you really intend going near the water, a pair of waders. Choose the waders carefully: tall waders on a short wally can cause a sawing action which is uncomfortable if not excruciating, though it does help with the ruptured mule bit.

Now for the mental re-arrangement, should it be necessary. (*Sun* readers can skip this bit.) You have to despise one or two things. Trade unions, workers, the out-of-work, students, woolly-minded liberals, socialists, Marxists, poofters, *Guardian* readers; those whose skin is pigmented black, brown or yellow, and all foreigners of whatever dermal hue. You favour the bringing back of cat, gallows, rack, thumbscrews and transportation. You demand summary execution of football hooligans, though you have a grudging admiration for the way they show the flag now and again by sacking towns populated entirely by dagos, wops or frogs.

Having sorted out your social attitudes, you can now concentrate on your attitudes to angling. Trout and salmon are the only fish fit for the attentions of a gentleman. Grayling? Waste of time, old boy. Neither one thing nor the other. Incredibly messy riser. Leave that to the cloth-capped chappies.

The cloth-capped chappies – i.e. coarse anglers – are well beyond the pale. Should you live next door to one, move. Or at least cease speaking to him forthwith. Should your sister have married one, cease speaking to her as well. And her cloth-capped brats.

Now you can specialise even further. Fly only for the old trout. None of those crude, weighted underwater lures. No wet flies, either. Dry fly... it's the only way to fish, an occupation for an officer and a gentleman ranking alongside fox hunting and pig sticking. By now you will have learned that the pronunciation is *dray flay*: as in *huntin'* and *stickin'*.

Should you actually have served in Her Majesty's armed forces, it helps the image, though it's no use confessing you were a lance-jack in the Catering Corps, a private in the Pay Corps, or wielded a nifty shovel with the Pioneers. Hint vaguely at a commission and refer to 'The Regiment', never 'The Mob' or 'The Shower'. That scar on your forehead? Old wound... don't really like to talk about it, old chap. It takes away some of the romance to admit that it was caused by a flying bottle during a NAAFI brawl in Catterick.

You're not well-britched enough to fish the classic dry fly waters – the Test, Itchen, Kennet – or even one of the less expensive chalk streams with the gin-clear water for which the dray flay was designed.

You can try the technique on the canal, but as you wade among the old bedsteads and bicycle frames, you can come in for some ill-natured barracking from those cloth-capped chappies you have sworn to avoid. Yobbos. Bloody Oiks.

But you can give it a go on the pound-a-fish ticket waters at the local trout farm, stocked with clapped-out brood fish or adolescent three-quarter-pounders surplus

You can try the technique on the canal...

to the local restaurant's requirements.

And a brave sight you make to be sure, wading thigh deep in the algae-clouded still water, flicking the old dray flay back and forth, stirring up the silt as you go. Often there's not a lot of success, mainly because the fish can't see the thing through the murk, but also because they're more used to the splashing of high-protein pellets as a signal that grub's up.

But try it late in May or early in June and you may catch Duffer's Fortnight, time of the suicidal mayfly hatches which even the dimmest of hand-fed fish recognise as feeding time. Get your fly in then, among the hatching flies smothering the surface - elbowing out of the way all the fellow wallies who have appeared from nowhere - and you'll doubtless cop for a couple of adolescent or geriatric trout.

Those are all you need. You can hold your head high in the wallypub as you slap your catch on the bar and announce modestly, 'Not bad, I suppose. Didn't give themselves up, though. With the old dray flay it's never easy. But nothing worth doing ever is, what?'

Try to be first in the pub. Otherwise you'll arrive to hear a fellow wally announcing, 'Not bad, I suppose. Didn't give themselves up, though. With the old dray flay...'

The nerve of some people. Pinching your lines...

Some Wally Appurtenances

Nothing is more heartbreaking than to spend your life acting like a wallyangler and not having your wallyness recognised. Perhaps it's because wallyangling is a specialised art form, recognisable to another angler, but to the outsider merely a symptom of common-or-garden insanity.

The answer is to advertise, to plaster yourself with wally appurtenances, to surround yourself with wally artifacts, so that even the dimmest will recognise you for what you are. The technique reaches its most specialised form in the Wallybadger (which see, for guidance on decoration of person and motor car) but long before you've got that far, even the most unperceptive would realise that you are a genuine and dedicated wally.

Your club badge, for a start, need not be displayed only once. Wear it on your lapel, on the breast pocket of your blazer or jacket and on your T-shirt. You can have the badge as a key-ring attachment, as cufflinks, and even embossed on your blazer buttons.

Fix one to your car's radiator grille and have stick-ons on the front and rear windscreens. Plaster it on every item of gear big enough to take it. By this time it should be fairly obvious that you are a devoted member of the Sludgethorpe Wallytonians, proud of your association with such a long-established and respected angling organisation.

Should your enthusiasm for the club be such as to colour all your other activities, you can even have the badge sewn on to your underpants. Its discovery by the object of your affections might hold up the proceedings a little, but at least it gives you something to talk about while things are warming up.

Personalised T-shirt slogans are a splendid means of advertising your wallyness, more so because you can compose them yourself. Simply send off your composition to the Wallyshirt Emporium, and back will come a selection of T-shirts announcing across the chest such sentiments as:

> I'M GAME – ARE YOU?
> FLY FISHERMEN DO IT STANDING UP
> HAPPINESS IS A ROD IN YOUR HAND
> I ALWAYS USE A BIG ONE
> MINE'S THE BIGGEST YOU'LL SEE TODAY
> I DIBBLE MY DROPPER
> MINE'S A WHOPPER
> I USUALLY *TIE* MY FLIES – BUT FOR YOU . . .

While you're at it, you could have some nonwally messages printed on the backs of the shirts to answer the questions posed by the bankside botherers: shame to waste the space. As you sit by the water with your back to the audience, anybody wishing to enquire after your luck, on the cadge, or wishing to pose some deep philosophical question, is answered by one or other of:

> NOT A TOUCH
> NARY A NIBBLE
> NOT A MAGGOT LEFT
> I'M USING MY LAST HOOK
> NO, I *DON'T* HAVE PATIENCE
> NO, I *WOULDN'T* LIKE IT
> IT DOESN'T HURT 'EM THAT MUCH
> I WANT TO BE ALONE
> BUGGER OFF

And don't forget angling ties. You can have tasteful, almost nonwally ones, with just the club badge or initials; standardwally ones depicting a fierce-looking fish, or naughtywally ones depicting a mermaid with big knockers.

*   *   *

You can get many wallypurtenances ABSOLUTELY FREE!!! by buying one of the angling magazines on the day it's including a free gift as a sales inducement. All the free gifts have two things in common – as well as being ABSOLUTELY FREE!!! they're also ABSOLUTELY USELESS!!!, which adds immensely to their wallyappeal.

Among popular gifts are:

A ring-end disgorger. Of which you already have six, only longer. This one would just about reach the tonsils of a stunted stickleback.

A plastic V-end for a rod rest, for which you need a bank stick, which does not come ABSOLUTELY FREE!!!

The smallest float in a range of floats, which would be used very rarely, even if you had the whole set. Correction – *especially* if you had the whole set.

An iron-on badge for your T-shirt. Gosh! The slogan on the badge is nothing more nor less than the name of the publication, and is given to you ABSOLUTELY FREE!!! in the hope that you'll be wally enough to wander around wearing it as a free ad.

A plastic key ring, also bearing the name of the publication; which name rubs off after four hours in the pocket. Still, it too is ABSOLUTELY FREE!!!

*   *   *

The wallyangler's interests are reflected in his home. It's amazing what you can do to a house to give it an atmosphere steeped in angling and to knock its market value right down.

It needs a name, for a start, so that people's curiosity is aroused as soon as they step through the front gate. So that they can ask, with the keenest interest, 'Why did you give your house a stupid name like that?'

The name can be evocative or nostalgic, such as *Bankside* or *Crook o' Lune*. It can indicate your continued interest in the Noble Art, as in *Anglinon, Stilcastin* or *Stilreelin*. It can evince hope, as in *Tight Lines* or *Fulcreel*. It can hint at an interest in particular fish, as in *Pike's Peak* or *Ruddanroach*. It can indicate a specialised interest in fly fishing, as in *Coch-y-Bondhu* or *Greenwell's Glory*. (If your favourite flies are Hairy Mary or Blanshard's Abortion, forget it.)

It is essential that you choose the name yourself. An angling wife, unless she were equally wally, on being asked to pick a name appropriate to her husband's pursuit and usual condition, would come up with something like *Notabite, Lyzalott, Nohope, Drynetts, Congapong* or *Pistagen*.

... Let's move into the house, admiring on the way the newly-installed stained glass window in the front door, depicting a leaping fish of enormous dimensions and violent hues, and see in what other ways the dedicated wally can impress his personality on the place.

Of course – there it is over the fireplace, a framed and embroidered sampler reading:

A FISHERMAN'S PRAYER

Lord, grant to me before I die
A fish so huge that even I,
When speaking of it afterwards,
Will never have the need to lie.

Originally, the *Fisherman's Prayer* was not overwally, but so often does it appear now that it ranks with the pokerwork mottos in the pub which read:

> *You don't have to be mad*
> *to work here*
> *- but it helps!*

And, talking about pokerwork mottos - here they are:

> *She was only an angler's daughter,*
> *But she'd swallow any old line.*

and

> *Definition of fishing: A line with a worm at both ends.*

The old 'uns are the best, eh?

Trophies are always a feature of a wally household, and there are few things uglier than a fishing trophy, unless you count darts and snooker trophies. Look at them... lining the mantelpiece and cluttering up the sideboard. Of *course*, a lot of the inscription plaques on them are blank. Trophies which are won lose a lot of their wallyness, and it can take time to build up a reasonable display. It's much quicker and wallier to buy the things.

Time to admire the china plates on the wall, depicting the anglers' favourite fish, one for each month of the year. Only three of them? That's because they're hand-painted by old English craftsmen in Taiwan and cost sixty quid apiece, delivered to your home one at a time every month. And by April the money had run out. Ah, well.

Food, eh? Served from dishes in the form of a fish. How very original. And the place mats: Thomas Bewick prints of old angling scenes. How tasteful. And what's the food being served? Ah... gudgeon, cooked to an original Izaak Walton recipe. How very - *groo!* Always a distinctive flavour with freshwater fish.

Before you go... a peep inside the wallyden. The inner sanctum. Holy of Holies. Where the real trophies are kept.

Ah... all those NO FISHING signs... ANGLING PROHIBITED... ANGLERS WILL BE PROSE-

CUTED... TICKET WATER ONLY... all nicked by our daredevil wally. And that large stuffed pike on the wall... almost certainly fought like a tiger, but the only struggle he had with it was getting it home from the jumble sale.

That's a nice fish – the blue marlin. Quite impressive, especially in that hard-fighting pose. Would be more impressive if it were more than eighteen inches long and wasn't made of plastic, but you can't have everything.

And those two pike skulls. One big, one small. The big one was a pike 100 years old, eh? And the small one? The same pike when it was only fifteen years old.

Ha! Get it! Joke, eh? You're certainly not as wally as you look, cracking jokes like that. Like it! Like it!

What? You're *not* joking? That's what the man said when you bought 'em?

Irish feller, was he? Yerss...

All In The Family

Many as the wallies are, and fast though they multiply, wallying can be a lonely business. Like every other pioneer, every original thinker, every trailblazer, your actions are often misunderstood or misrepresented. You are subject to verbal and physical abuse, ejected from nonwally pubs, disbarred from nonwally clubs and generally ostracised by the hard core of unthinking antiwallies.

Don't despair. A simple, immediate and highly effective remedy for your solitary state is at hand under your own roof: The Family. A family that wallies together, jollies together, as the Bard so rightly observed. And there's nothing like family fishing for cementing the wallybonds that bind you; nothing like the company of your Nearest and Dearest under God's clear sky; nothing like the silvery laughter of your wife and little ones to lift the spirits and disperse the tedium of the day.

Let us assume that yours is a nuclear family: wife, two children and mother-in-law. (Mother-in-law *is* part of the nuclear family, if only under the heading of poisonous waste.) The mother-in-law is essential to the success of a wallyouting; without her it wouldn't be half as wally. Not forgetting, either, the wallydog, who will go absolutely berserk with joy at being out in the open where the wild things are.

A wallyfamily outing calls for a few changes in the routine. No longer is it possible, in the selfish old way, just to pull on a few old clothes and lurch out unshaven into the dawn. There are other people to consider.

Wifey busies herself in the kitchen preparing the sandwiches – cress, tomato, cucumber and pressed chicken roll – carefully cutting off the crusts and quartering the rounds. You collect all the crockery and cutlery for the hamper – the cardboard plates, cups and saucers; plastic knives and forks; tubes of mustard and mayonnaise – and fill the family-sized thermos flasks with tea, coffee, and cream-of-chicken soup. Not forgetting the disposable tablecloth and the paper-tissue napkins in tasteful pastel colours.

While the kids are tucking in to their vitamin-enriched cornflakes, you go out to clean the car. A clean car is essential for a wallyfam outing. Even though, by the time you get to the water, it will be as mud-spattered as every other car, that's not the point. No wally worth his salt would set out *en famille* in a car that wasn't sparkling.

The freshly-swabbed boot of the car is packed with hampers, stools, umbrellas, windbreaks, spare clothes for the kids in case the weather changes; a set of extra scarves, cardigans and blankets for mother-in-law, and mother-in-law's medicine chest just in case she has one of her turns.

Right. The car's packed and you're ready. No, you're *not* ready. You're not going out in that windcheater you wore last week. Go and put on that new one from C & A, the cream one with the smart blue piping and the badge depicting a leaping dolphin. Change those trousers while you're at it; put on your beige gaberdines. And don't wear those awful wellingtons: change into those comfortable Marks & Spencer slip-ons.

Ready, children? Children? Where've they got to? Oh dear, they've been down at the compost heap, digging worms. After what they were told last night. Just look at the state of them! Straight upstairs and get changed!

Now you – yes, *you*, Cloth Ears – while you're waiting, you'd better brush the dog down as well. Can't have it coming into the car like that. Apart from the compost all over him, there's mother's chest to consider.

Ah, yes. Mother. Where is she? Now stop fussing; she's just had to go to the toilet again. You know how she gets when she's excited.

*　　*　　*

In less than three hours you're ready for off, held up only slightly at the end because mother-in-law had to go back upstairs for another one. You know how she gets when she's excited.

Now then. Choice of venue. The lateness of the day, the numbers involved, and other factors such as the mother-in-law not being able to walk more than a hundred yards before her palpitations set in, do rule out some of the better fishing spots. Not that it matters all that much; fishing being incidental to a true wallyfamily outing.

The route has to be considered carefully, too, based on the number of garages – ideally one every two miles – with loos comfortable and sophisticated enough to cope with mother-in-law's emergency stops. You know how she gets when she's excited.

The ideal wallyspot should be no more than fifty yards from the road or car park, preferably one containing a loo; just upstream of a fishing match in progress; and slap in the middle of a well-used footpath or towpath. A properly organised wallyfamily on a good day can cause more obstruction than a fleet of flying pickets on a motorway slip road.

Right, so we fish here. No, we don't. It's too windy for mother.

OK ... we fish here. No, we don't. Those trees will keep all the sun off.

Over here? No. It means mother will have to walk back up that slope every time she wants to go. You know how she gets...

This do? Suppose so. It's not ideal, but we don't want to

97

get any closer to those men along there. Never knew there'd be so many out today. The language... really! I hope you're going to speak to them if they keep using words like that.

Mother-in-law gets settled down in her orthopaedic camping armchair, tucked into her foot muff and wrapped in several layers of thermal insulation. Now we can get tackled up.

Oh no, we can't. There's all that picnic stuff to be unpacked yet. Hope those awful men don't come trampling all over it. That's it, put the folding table here. Yes, in the middle of the path. Can't be helped: it's too steep anywhere else.

Wallykids tackle up, put floats on upside-down and reels wrong way round. Wallydad unships their gear and puts everything back the right way. He's about to tackle up himself when, 'Ugh! Beastly maggots. I can't put these on. Dad! Will you put this maggot on the hook for me, please?'

'No – me first, Daddy! Ladies first! Sugar and spice and all things – Ow! Did you see what he did to me, Daddy?'

Wallydad gets both kids sorted out and baited up; gets tackled up himself and ready for the first cast, when 'Yoo-hoo! Will you take mother up to the toilets, please? No, I can't take her myself, these stilettos keep sinking in the grass. I *know* I should have put my flats on, but they don't go with this coat.'

Shuffle up to loo with mother-in-law. Slowly. At mother-in-law pace, which is that of a sick, three-toed sloth. After prolonged wait outside Ladies, shuffle even more slowly back: she's in no hurry now. Bung mother-in-law back into chair to be re-swaddled by wife. And here we go... first cast of the –

'Yoo-hoo, everybody! Dinner is served! Ha ha. Come and *get* it...

All those delicious cress-and-cucumber sandwiches. So dainty. Such a change from the usual old cheese-and-pickle doorstops. And that refreshing coffee and chicken cup-a-soup. So much better for one than all the usual old lager and scotch. Steady, children … not so fast which that Instant Yuckywhip Topping. Don't want to upset your stomachs.

What an enjoyable break in the fishing. Not that any fishing's happened yet, but just you wait. Pity about all those wasps and bluebottles and midges. Something ought to be done about them.

… Even as we speak, the little woman's whipped out her aerosol. There we are, now. Everything's had a good spraying, including the sandwiches, and there's not a live insect in sight. Plenty of dead ones, or those kicking their last in the trifle, but that's part of the price of the open-air life.

That was delicious, my pet. Now, back to the – What? Let the dog out?

Yes. Let the dog out. Comes the Moment of Truth. The Point of No Return. Time to Stand Up and Be Counted.

You're either a wally or you're not. Temptation beckons at every turn to give up all pretensions to wallyness. And if you crack now – if you leave the dog where it is, if you order the kids to behave themselves or ELSE, if you tell the wife to clear up and shut up, if you offer mother-in-law life membership of Exit, if you restore order and quiet and get on with your fishing – you've failed totally as a wally.

But you're made of sterner stuff. You've not spent the best years of your life practising to be a wallyangler for nothing. Definitely not. The Resolute Approach, that's the thing.

So, striding purposefully to the car, you open the door and let out wallydog. The Hound of the Wallyvilles. A small step for you, but a giant step for wallykind.

* * *

A word here about wallydog. Anybody who takes his dog fishing is by definition a wally. Any dog which is allowed to accompany him is therefore by definition a wallydog.

But there are wallydogs and wallydogs. And yours has to be something special.

There is no place here for gentle, sensible dogs who will sit quietly on the bank – bored out of their skulls, perhaps, but quietly – asking no more than the occasional pat on the head and a piece of cheese from the baitbox. Dogs who will do no more than give an appreciative wag of the tail when master catches a fish; they're no good. That is wallydogging at its most passive, least demanding. Shows a definite lack of canine wallyspirit.

Real angling wallydogs are chosen for their special qualities; for lineage and conditioning which bring out their full potential. The dogs can be:

Big. Nothing like bulk for spreading terror along the bank. A good big 'un, such as an Irish wolfhound, mastiff, Rhodesian ridgeback, Pyrenean mountain dog or common-or-garden Alsatian: nothing like 'em for scattering groundbait, maggot tins and rod rests. A big wallydog on a good day can wreck the tackle and ruin the prospects of up to 200 matchfishers.

Small. Pekes, Yorkies, dachshunds, corgis, Scotties, can reach the parts other wallydogs cannot reach. Diving under stools, leaping into bait cans, wrapping themselves in landing nets, racing in circles around pursuing anglers. There's no end to the endearing tricks they can get up to.

Silent and slobbery. This mainly applies to the big ones who have the height to creep up behind a seated angler just as he's keyed up to strike, and give him a big, slobbering kiss behind the ear. This causes instant disorientation: from the force of the lick and the passionate heavy breathing, he knows instantly that it's not the wife.

Booming. Again, it's often the big ones. Crashing quickly down the bank to let off a Baskerville roar at close range that sends the angler leaping screaming into the water. The basset hound is a low-slung exception to the height qualification, letting off a monster-type roar at the level of a seated angler's naughty bits that has him hitting the water even quicker.

Yappy and snappy. These qualities often go together. Half an hour of non-stop yapping can cause an angler to indicate his displeasure by braining the thing with the landing net handle. Not an entirely wise thing to do, as the dog indicates its displeasure by nipping in smartly and taking a chunk out of his leg.

Ravening. Wallydogs on the loose will eat anything – preferably anglers' butties, left incautiously on the bank – but they'll cheerfully see off groundbait, cheese, bread, maggots and even worms.

Burrowing. This wallydog re-discovers his old terrier instincts and digs holes all over the place, backheeling clods of grass and soil over any angler within range and sending longer-distance clods splashing into carefully groundbaited swims. When all other likely digging places have been exhausted it will scientifically undermine the angler's basket, thus ensuring that he finishes the next strike flat on his back.

Aquatic. Wallydogs have a higher than normal percentage of seal in their genetic make-up, and love nothing better than taking to the water, often encouraged by the sticks which wallymaster throws in. On retrieving the stick they will not swim directly back with it, but will paddle determinedly up or down stream, through the lines of as many anglers as they can before tiring of the fun. On emerging from the water they give an energetic shake which on average soaks 3.5 anglers to the skin, before bounding back to wallymaster and knocking over a dozen bait cans in the process. Aquatic wallydogs are usually the hairier ones, with coats holding anything up to three gallons of canal water, and which definitely make a shake worth the shaking.

*　　*　　*

...Back to the Family Wally, who have now settled down,

blocking the towpath to all but a 50-ton tank.

Mother-in-law has been shifted for the tenth time, into a spot which is neither too hot, too cold, too sunny, too shady, too windy or too muggy. Sitting in a fug of Vick and Thermogene which, as well as being good for her chest, is keeping the flies off, she grumpily knocks hell out of a box of Milk Tray.

Wallywife sits in a folding chair, anointing her arms with sun lotion and dabbing camomile lotion on her nose, listening to a selection of tapes by Barry Manilow, Julio Iglesias, The Carpenters, Demis Roussos and Max Bygraves. Not all of which are to the taste of the match anglers, if the shouts of 'Turn that bloody thing off!' are anything to go by.

You, as Wallydad, stand in the sunlight on the bank, clad in a dazzling white sweater, waving a rod varnished to a high-gloss finish, wondering why the fish are being so shy today. Something to do with all those oafish matchmen, you shouldn't wonder.

Wallykids have by now given up all pretence of fishing, having little left to do it with now that they've lost most of their terminal tackle in the trees behind them, or on the underwater snags in front of them. Most of their bait has been stuffed down each other's neck, they've fallen in the water three times apiece, they've run out of stones to pelt the ducks with, and they're bored with beating each other up.

Nothing for it but for you to lay your rod down and organise some jolly sports events along the bank. Wallykids are beaten in the 100-metre sprint by wallydog and return sniffling after the sixth event on account of being given a thick ear each by those horrid men down there.

Over to the matchmen you stride, determined to avenge the injuries inflicted on your young. Returning with a few contusions on your person, which you are unwilling and unable to avenge on account of the size and numbers of the opposition, but at least with the satisfaction of having told *them* a thing or two.

'Never mind, dear,' says Missis Wally, by way of comfort. 'Just you have some of these nice vol-au-vents and forget all about those bullies. Shouldn't be allowed, men like that.'

After the vol-au-vents, you toss up whether to have one more try at the fish, but the sun has started to dip behind the trees and the evening rise of midges is penetrating mother-in-law's Vick-and-Thermogene fug. What's more, her leg is playing up; a medically baffling condition, as she hasn't used it much all day, but one which indicates she's had enough.

So it's time to pack up. Leaving the kids' terminal tackle where it has been snagged, and the bank well-strewn with non-biodegradable wrappings and artifacts. It always takes longer than you think to pack up and, despite what's left behind on the bank, there always seems more to bring back than you took with you; a well-known wallylaw of any family day out.

But finally you make it, and the car glides smoothly back home. The inside smells of an enticing compound of mud, slime, expiring algae, mother-in-law's Vick, damp dog and the kids' regurgitated vol-au-vents.

You feel a quiet glow of satisfaction because you've succeeded. Against all opposition, fighting all temptation, you've made it a real wallyday out. That night, in the wallypub over a half of cooking, you'll be able to tell your fellow Rotarians all about it.

You've made a stand for the good old family values. Done something to redress the balance; something to correct the image of the angler as a loner, a misanthrope. And to re-affirm the truth of the old adage: there's more to fishing than catching fish.

Wallies At Sea

As a dedicated wally, you have a mission in life, which is to brighten up the scene for those around you. And a sea fishing trip gives you the ideal opportunity. Without your contribution, the other anglers would just board a boring old boat, cross some boring old bits of sea and catch some boring old fish. They may think, in their ignorance, that they're enjoying themselves. But it needs you to add the extra sparkle to the trip, to make it an outing to remember, to provide the fun they've been missing all their lives

But first, you've got to look after Number One. Public spirited though you are, you owe it to yourself to ensure that you get the most out of the trip by catching fish in as much comfort as circumstances will allow.

The important thing is to get a position at the stern. From there, you need do no accurate casting to avoid tangling the lines of others and you are protected from the spray which comes over the bows. The breakfasts of those amidships, which tend to emerge as soon as the boat hits any kind of broken water, fly harmlessly past and add to the attraction for the fish.

To be sure of a position at the stern, it is essential to board the boat first. You can do it the polite, civilised and orderly way by arriving first. Or you can do it one of the wallyways, which are much more fun, more frequently successful, and hold none of the boredom or inconvenience.

As the boarding starts, shout loudly from the bank,

The important thing is to get a position at the stern...

'Gangway! Gangway! Make way there for a man with a wooden leg!'

As the procession halts, nip smartly to the front, rod case clutched crutchwise under your armpit. Hop on one leg up the gangplank, shouting, 'Thank 'ee, Jim lad! Thank 'ee koind sirs! Old Long John won't forget 'ee when the toime comes! Oh arr...'

Those you have just clumped past may react by falling about in hysterical laughter, thinking what a wag you are. They may, but so far they never have. Do not be surprised if they respond with churlish abuse and later attempt to throw you overboard.

A less obtrusive and more socially acceptable way is to help the old age pensioner who is being allowed on the boat first. If he's not being allowed on first - which is a reflection on the callous and disrespectful attitudes of your fellow men - steer him swiftly from the back with cries of, 'Make way for a Senior Citizen, folks! Age before beauty!' Grasp him firmly by the elbow, take his rods from him, and support him in safety onto the boat. From then on he's on his own.

'Pick where you like, Pop,' you cry, kindly draping his rods back around him, and leaving him to be trampled by those behind in the dash for the stern.

Should he be spry enough to attempt a foot race to dispute your prior claim, or be ungrateful enough to protest in any way, take firm but necessary measures such as shoving him into the scuppers or kicking his stick from under him.

... Boarding a boat from the beach calls for a modified but not dissimilar technique, involving as it does a ladder which is slung over the side and hooked to the bulwarks.

If the foot of the ladder is not to be left swinging free, it has to be held firm; a task which, in the usual absence of any able-bodied seafaring person, falls to the first angler in the queue. Make sure it's not you. Not only is this a thankless task, if only because nobody ever stops shoving long enough to thank you, but you end up by being last on board and soaked to the naughty bits.

Once the ladder has been grasped, usually by some caring person who has never been sea fishing before, you can safely jump the queue with a helpful cry of 'Watch your bul'arks!' While he's glancing down, wondering if his flies are undone, you can mount the ladder and claim your place.

The Senior Citizen routine can work here as well, though the old boy's hesitation at having to splash through the incoming waves may give other less principled people a chance to barge in and assist him aboard ahead of you. So here you must modify the procedure by leading from the front. Scramble aboard, with a cry of, 'Allow me!', then yank the old boy up the ladder after you.

Once you're aboard, you have no real need of the old lad and can safely dispose of him.

So why, you may ask, should you help him up instead of dashing straight for the stern. Good point. But (a) he's your excuse for jumping the queue, and (b) you need something to leave at the top of the ladder to impede the progress of anybody trying to dispute your claim.

*   *   *

Once you've recovered your composure, you can indulge in some of the wally activities which add to the spice of danger inherent in every sea trip.

When you've chopped up your bait, leave it lying around where people can slip in it: that's always good for a laugh. (See 'The End-of-the-Pier Show' for detailed instructions.)

Many sea fish have spines that can inflict painful and potentially septic wounds, but any Tom, Dick or Harry can pick up the run-of-the-mill punctures or scratches. Wally goes in for honourable scars much more spectacular than these.

When a big conger is hauled inboard, do not leave it to

the skipper to dispatch, but leap in for the kill yourself, lunging at it with your high-grade, tempered steel Bowie knife, which you bought at the wallytackle shop specially for such an occasion. As the conger bucks and thrashes, bring your knife down in keen-eyed wallyfashion through the back of your left hand or the skipper's gumboot.

Dismiss all those silly stories about the conger's ferocity and tenacity of life. Liven up quiet moments by rummaging through the sack of eels to lift them out and admire your catch. If you can retrieve your finger stumps, put them in a plastic bag and keep them in a safe place until you get ashore. They can do wonders with microsurgery these days.

On the way back, with all the rods inboard, there'll be time and opportunity for your renowned ventriloquist act. Grip a dead conger firmly by the back of the neck, sit it on your knee and ask, 'And what's your name, little man?' You might even get the chance to swivel its head and answer 'Eli' – without the slightest movement of your lips – before the conger demonstrates that it's not as dead as it looks. What it does to your nose might be initially distressing, but it will at least ensure you're never troubled by blackheads or pimples again.

Other wally things you can do with sea fish, assuming you've the appendages left to do them with, include:

Grabbing a live and spinning dogfish with your bare hands. This effectively demonstrates the abrasive qualities of its skin, regarded highy enough in cabinet-making circles to be used as super-grade sandpaper.

Observing what a nice little fish is the whiting, and poking a finger in its mouth to examine more closely its delicate dentition.

Learning to differentiate between the thornback ray and the stingray. The thornback's the one with thorn-shaped spines down its back. The stingray's got a spike – only one, but highly poisonous – sticking up from its tail. An experienced wally can tell the difference blindfold.

Warning everybody not to touch the deadly spines of

the nasty little weever which has just been landed. Then stamping on it in your plimsolls or rope-soled sandals.

* * *

When the boat is travelling between marks, with the rods inboard, or during lulls between bites, it's your chance to entertain the whole company with your side-splitting seafaring jokes and comedy routines. You should never board a boat without packing a plastic parrot for the Long John Silver bit, and a pair of eyepatches for the Admiral Nelson sketch. Captain Bligh doesn't need a lot in the way of props; just practise sticking your hands behind your back and barking, 'Mestah Chrestian!'

You can do the Admiral Nelson bit before you even leave harbour by way of a warm-up. Donning an eyepatch and sticking one arm under your coat, stride up and down the deck declaring, 'Eye eye! Don't worry folks – I'm 'armless!' Then you clap on the second eyepatch, stare blindly around the crowded harbour and declare, 'I see no ships!'

These quips, screamingly funny though they are, do not always get the laughs they deserve; often the fate of the more subtle jokes in front of a stone-cold audience. So you may have to switch to the broader music-hall stand-up jokes such as, 'Cap'n – I can't see the mizzen mast. Don't tell me it's mizzen!'

Make the routine jokes about sharp ends, blunt ends, splicing the mainbrace and looking for the golden rivet. Though the skipper has possibly heard these before, he will receive them with the appreciation due to the Good Old Good Ones and applaud your performance with a merry shout of 'Pillock!'

From pillock, it's but a short step to pollack. Learn to recognise a pollack when you see one. This member of the cod family is good for hours of jokes on its name.

When somebody turns round and asks, 'What are these fish we're catching?', give vent to a couple of bars of

Colonel Bogey. When he's standing there, looking puzzled, shout, 'Pollacks – and the same to you!' Upon which he will fall about with uncontrollable laughter. Or still stand there looking totally mystified, in which case you'll have to repeat the joke until he gets it. Some people can be incredibly thick.

When a fish slips out of somebody's grasp and goes bouncing across the deck, you can come in, quick as a flash, with, 'Hey up! You've dropped a pollack!' You can repeat this one several times, just to make sure people have got it. And if anybody laughs, repeat it again.

You may be lucky enough to have a fellow wally on board, who will slip you the feed lines of the tried-and-trusted wallyfishing jokes:

'I say, this fish has no nose!'

'That fish has no nose? How does it smell?'

'Terrible.'

'I say! Can you kipper secret?'

'I'm a dab hand at that, but you'll have to speak up, old boy. I'm a bit hard of herring.'

''Pon my sole! You're codding me!'

'No need to get crabby, old son. Just remember your plaice . . .'

And when the congers start to be pulled aboard, prepare to greet one with an appropriate song: *Eel Meet Again . . . Fangs for the Memory . . . Eel Eye Addio . . . Tie Me Conger Eel Down, Sport . . .*

Don't worry about boring the audience. You can tell when they've had enough by the way they hit you with dead fish or stuff live congers down your trousers.

*　　*　　*

When the boat hits rough water, a lot of people may start to feel unwell. This is as good a time as any for the Long John Silver routine. Cheers people up no end, it does. As they hang over the side, bidding farewell to their Weetabix, or lie in the scuppers turning a tasteful shade of green, clump around with parrot akimbo roaring, 'Arr, Jim lad! Them as dies'll be the lucky ones!'

Those whom you encouraged earlier to over-indulge in the Demon Drink with exhortations of, 'Get it down – it'll do you good!', you can now advise, 'Get it up – it'll do you good!'

Do your rounds of the boat, munching a double-decker sandwich or a hunk of pizza, swigging from a can of fizzy lager and belching noisily in appreciation. Stop at each green-faced wreck by the rail and offer a bite or a swig to settle his stomach. Better still, tip a carton of diced vegetable salad into your hand and ask, 'Here y'are, old son. Is this yours?' Be ready to sidestep any sudden and involuntary reaction.

*　　*　　*

So far we've assumed that you are one of the cast-iron wallies who can go through a sea trip wolfing down junk food and swigging the hard or fizzy stuff. But you may be one whose stomach is as queasy as the next man's, and ready to throw up at the first suggestion of a ripple under the keel.

Remember that, despite your sufferings, you are bound by the Wallyoath not to waste all that good breakfast, pigging it as you did on sausage, bacon, egg, tomatoes, black pudding and fried bread. It is incumbent upon you to add some texture to the lives of your fellow men and to ensure that, however much you're suffering, you're not suffering alone.

So leave your position at the stern, whence you could throw up the livelong day with little distress to yourself and no inconvenience to anybody else. Make your rounds of the ship and do your duty.

Stagger up to the bow and from there work your way back down the ship, throwing up as you progress and making sure that every heave finds its mark. Try it over the side, close to and upwind of a fellow angler, ensuring that he gets a good spattering; do it in bait tins; on often-used portions of the deck where anyone still on his feet is bound to step in it; over lunch boxes and sandwich packets; in any hats you find lying about, and in the pockets of discarded anoraks. (*Un*discarded anoraks if you can manage it: you get extra wallypoints for that.)

If you see anybody struggling manfully and successfully to hold back his breakfast, step up and deposit some of your own close by him; if possible, *on* him. That should set him off nicely.

By the time you've got back to the stern, all passions will be spent, your stomach will be empty, you'll be feeling a lot better. Which is more than can be said for those near whom, next to whom or upon whom you've thrown up.

*   *   *

Perhaps you've had a fishless or disappointing trip and have failed to do yourself any damage at all. Don't despair. There's still time. Warm up on the way back by swigging down a bottle of rum and entertaining everyone with your immortal rendition of *The Good Ship Venus*.

As the ship berths, bid everyone a hearty farewell and step athletically over the side. First, as always.

'You're supposed to wait for the gangplank!' calls the skipper. '*Pillock*...'

Some Side-Splitting Wallyjapes: 3

Angling provides lots of jolly and horrific things to slip into your mates' beer. Choose the Guinness drinkers for preference: they don't notice the presence of any foreign bodies in the dark liquid until they've supped their way almost to the bottom.

Maggots, worms, tadpoles, frogs, toads... they're all guaranteed to have everybody falling about helpless with laughter. But the best of all, if you can find one, is a freshwater crayfish. Not only is it, at close quarters, ugly enough to frighten the pants off anybody, but there's always the chance, as it slides down towards the rim of the glass, that it will grab your mate's nose in its pincers.

Oh, what a lark! As he's standing there saying, 'I duppode you dig dad's bluddy fuddy,' you can riposte with, 'That's you all over. Can't keep your nose out of anything. Har har.' Ooh, you are a card.

With frogs, slimy and athletic as they are, there's always the danger of their being swallowed. Actually, there are frog-swallowing contests, which are very wally things to do, but there you're up against some stiff competition. A citizen of Market Drayton, Poddy the Poacher as he was known in piscatorial and constabulary circles, was cleared some years ago by the local magistrates of a charge of cruelty by swallowing live frogs. He'd swallowed the frogs all right, but his solicitor defended the action by saying that it was no worse than using them as livebait for pike, which is another very wally thing to do.

Poddy, too, was not just scoffing the frogs – he washed them down with Guinness, by the way, which was no doubt some small consolation to them – just for the wallyness of it. Oh, no. He was attempting to beat the then current frog-swallowing record of five in sixty-five seconds, held by an Irishman called McNamara. Whether he succeeded or not is a fact lost in the mists of time, the better-class record books having eschewed publicity for any wallyrecords likely to cause distress to under-privileged amphibians, and the author currently short of the fare to Market Drayton to pursue such a piece of totally useless knowledge.

Even Poddy and the redoubtable Mr McNamara have a long way to go before they can equal the feat of one Mac Norton, known on the wallyfringes of showbusiness as The Human Aquarium, who once swallowed three gallons of water and twenty-five live frogs in one go.

... We digress. There stands your mate, aghast at having seen something large and slimy materialise from the bottom of his glass and having felt it slide swiftly down his throat.

'What the hell was that?'

'Looked like a frog. Or was it a toad?'

'Omygawd! What shall I do?'

'Only one thing for it, old son – hop it!'

... Pub landlords on the whole are not in favour of hilarious goings-on such as these, the average pub landlord not being noted for his sense of humour. They do seem to get upset at the sight of paying customers throwing up and rushing screaming from the pub. They are sensitive, too, about the occasional outbreaks of wallybattering which take place after the misfiring of an otherwise mirth-provoking wallyjape. It's not so much the battering they mind. It's cleaning the blood off the wallpaper and sweeping the teeth off the carpet.

What a Picture . . .

Half the pleasure of angling is in reminiscing, looking back on the season's triumphs in your photograph album.

No need to wait until the end of the season, either – or even the end of the day. With polaroid shots you can bore first, bore fast, with pictures of fish that your mates saw caught only ten minutes ago.

But we're talking now about proper pictures, taken with expertise and loving care and using genuine wally-techniques.

The Bulging Net shot is a favourite, assuming you ever catch enough fish to fill a keepnet: though in Ireland, or even in England on a newly-stocked water, you may pull in enough fish to fill a couple of nets.

Hope for a bright, sunny day for it, so that the fish will really look something with the glare of the sun on their scales.

For the first twenty or so shots, drag the nets out on to the bank, bulging and rippling, with the sheen of the fish showing through. Drag them back to the water and out again whenever the authentic bulging and rippling starts to fade. If you've come prepared, you'll have a tripod and remote control apparatus among your gear. If not, you'll have to rely on your mates or passers-by to operate the camera.

Sit yourself between the nets for a couple of end-on shots. Then turn the nets sideways, open ends to each other, with yourself in between again. Then a few shots from above. Then some shots of you lifting up first one net, and then the other.

You can use another roll or two of film with the fish out of the nets and spread in rows along the bank. Always tricky, this, with the damn things jumping about, refusing to keep still until they've tired a bit or coughed themselves to a standstill.

Now for the bigger specimens, pictured individually. Hold them up by the tail for starters. Now hold them up horizontally in front of you, just under your chin. Now in white hunter pose, one hand holding up the fish, the forefinger of the other hand pointing at it.

Lay the bigger specimens out singly on the grass against some point of comparison: a matchbox, a 5p piece, a foot rule, a bait tin (small for preference), an unconscious mate (ditto).

There are several wallyexpressions recommended for the pictures: modest but proud, stern and triumphant, daft and dribbling, gormless and gloating. Then a few others for laughs: with your teeth out, your glasses on upside down, your baseball cap on sideways, your bobbly hat pulled over your eyes, your trousers rolled up and a knotted hanky over your head.

If you live near enough, nip back home and change. You look much better in that nice white Aran sweater than in those drab old fishing togs.

Hook the bigger fish again for action replays of the capture, putting plenty of strain on the rod so that it bends double through most of its length. Then a few shots of the landing, swishing the net up and down in the water to get the effect of the spray glinting in the sun.

If you can afford it, you needn't stop at still photographs. A cine or video camera can record the whole thing for posterity, and you can get much more mileage out of the playing and landing scenes, even a few shots of the float bobbing and diving wildly as the re-hooked fish tries to make for cover. And for action comedy, a few shots of you walking with the fish along the top of a dry stone wall, or letting it flop back into the water and diving in after it.

The fish won't look too clever after all this. Quite a number of them will float away belly-up after you've put them back. But they'll be all right: a few minutes in the sun never did a fish any harm. Nor being bounced around in a landing net for ten minutes. Survival of the fittest. Bet they enjoyed it, really. Made a bit of a mess of the keepnets, though, with all those scales they left inside.

It's only natural that you'll want wider publicity than you can get by showing the pictures in the pub or having movie sessions at home. Overcoming your natural modesty, you'll send off a few snaps to the local paper and angling press.

And they'll appear. Perhaps not in the angling press, but you know what that's like. Bloody mafia. Only publish photographs of their mates. But in the local paper - hey, a half-page spread, headlined: WILLY'S WHOPPERS!

And look at the caption 'Local angler Willy Wally, 35-year-old saggermaker's bottom knocker of Potbank Road, Sludgethorpe, struck it rich on his latest outing. Not for Willy the ones that got away. He's pictured here with his bulging nets after a personal best catch of 150lb of bream and roach. And, below, he's taking a closer look at the fish - all 64 of them - as they bask in the beautiful July sunshine of last weekend. Well done, Willy! Sludgethorpe is proud of you!'

It takes a bit of the shine off things next day when there's a knock on the door and the local RSPCA inspector is standing there with a copy of the local paper in his hand. A bit more when the paper's letters page the following week is full of angry missives headed WICKED WILLY!; STOP THIS MANIAC!; DOWN WITH ANGLING! and HOW WOULD HE LIKE IT?

And there's no shine left at all when the club secretary gets a letter from the owners of the water telling him that in view of the adverse publicity, the club's concession on the water is cancelled as of this date.

Bloody spoilsports. Jealousy, that's all it is. Can't bear to see people doing better than themselves. I mean, just look at this one...

The Good Wallypub Guide

Within staggering distance of every stretch of water are fishermen's pubs. Some are just plain, cosy, comfortable and warm, with sturdy wooden furniture; stone, tiled or wood floors; roomy enough for fully-laden anglers to fit into, or with an alcove for stacking the tackle. The beers are drinkable, often local. The food is plain and wholesome, with not a tame trout on the menu and nothing in a basket. Stuffed fish on the walls are few, unspectacular and have been caught locally. The name of the pub is traditional but nothing special: *Rose and Crown, White Hart, Three Horseshoes, George and Dragon, Wagon and Horses.*

These pubs are not for the wally. The landlords or the breweries have obviously failed to realise the wally-potential of the hostelries, have done nothing to improve their image or wallyappeal.

But thankfully, there are other pubs about which *have* been improved, where the wally feels immediately at home, and where he can relax in an atmosphere redolent of wallyangling.

Nor are the pubs difficult to track down. The name is usually enough. The *Izaak Walton*, for starters. Or *Izaac* or *Isaac*. As the old buffer seldom spelt his own name the same twice in a row – it was *Izaac* on his marriage lines, *Izaak* on his will, and *Isaac* on his tombstone – who's to quibble?

There *are* Izaak Walton pubs which have been called such for two or three hundred years. These are likely to be nonwally or superwally: either pubs used by normal anglers or patronised by anglers whose families have been wallies for two or three hundred years. Anglers whose families have been wallies for two or three hundred years do not take kindly to the incursion of novice or aspiring wallies. But old-established Izaak Walton pubs are few and far between compared with the number of Izaak Waltons which, only a few years ago, slaked local thirsts under the signs of *Dog and Duck, Pig and Whistle* or *Railwayman's Arms*.

There are other great angling names of the past which could be applied to pubs, but what wally would recognise the *Charles Cotton* or the *Dame Juliana* as having anything to do with fishing? No, with the *Izaak Walton*, you're on a pretty safe bet.

Even safer are *The Jolly Fisherman, The Fisherman's Rest, The Happy Angler, The Singing Reel, The Bulging Creel, The Leaping Trout*. Now we're really getting somewhere, with a set of names rarely likely to lead to disappointment.

One early guide is to be found on the wall outside: a notice reading, ANGLERS ARE KINDLY REQUESTED TO USE THE PUBLIC BAR. This emphasises that the landlord caters for wallies of every persuasion, and does not wish to upset the non-angling wallies in the saloon.

If, on the way through the public bar, you bang your head on the half-dozen lobster pots and glass lobster pot floats hanging from the ceiling, and get entangled in the tastefully draped lengths of trawl netting, you can be reasonably sure you've chosen well. Especially if the pub is fifty miles from the sea.

When your eyes become accustomed to the gloom, for wallypubs are often in semi-darkness – both for atmosphere and to prevent the dust on the lobster pots from becoming too obvious – you will notice other aspects of the decor which confirm your original findings.

There'll be baskets along the wall, usually old game-fishing creels, a highly encouraging sign if the pub overlooks the Grand Union Canal. And there will be the odd fly rod hanging on brackets, fitted up with an early fixed-spool reel, a braided sea line and a pike spoon.

Now we're really getting somewhere, but for a final check, inspect the many fish in glass cases around the walls. They may be cracked and old, with scales missing and fins fraying, but gad, they don't catch fish like these any more. Look at the dates on some of them: 1888, 1897, 1903, 1912 . . . adding up to a glorious historical pageant of fishing hereabouts, which is all the more interesting as the pub wasn't built until 1934.

Rub the dust off the plaques on some of the cases and read the details of the catches. River Dee, River Tay, River Shannon, Lough Erin. And contributions from the Hooghly, Zambezi, Limpopo and Orinoco. Imagine the dedication of those anglers, bringing their trophies all the way to rest in a pub seven miles outside Watford. And those fascinating labels on the side of the cases . . . Lot 82, Lot 135, Lot 683.

Those framed sepia photographs on the walls. All those sturdy old boys in whiskers and tweeds, clutching fish of enormous size. Locals all, no doubt. What do the captions say? Edinburgh . . . Heidelburg . . . Chittagong . . . Rangoon . . .

You can settle down now and enjoy yourself. You've found your pub all right.

Address mine host in extrovert wallyspeak, slapping your thigh in swashbuckling fashion to indicate that you're a man of action who's spent all morning braving the elements.

'Bit breezy out there today, old chap. Nearly took off once or twice. Like bloody Mary Poppins, what? Certainly didn't do the fishing much good, with the water whipped up like that. Could hardly see the old float for the spray.'

'Oh, arr,' he replies in his best Bethnal Green rustic. 'You're not the first as has said it. Fishing the lock near the plastics factory, were 'ee? Notorious, that is. Might ha' bin better off down by the paperworks. But pay no mind, sir. There's as good fish in there as ever came out. Now then, what's your pleasure?'

'A pint of your best, I think, landlord. None of this plastic rubbish. What do you recommend?'

'After a hard mornin' like this, sir, I'd say a glass of Old Izaak's Nutbrown Country Ale. Straight from the barrel.'

Up it comes. Old Izaak's Nutbrown Country Ale. Brewed in Birmingham. Straight from the barrel, via the natty electric pump with a handle topped by a large plastic acorn or small plastic coconut.

Time for some grub. Feel a bit peckish after all that activity. What's on the menu? Fish pie? Seafood platter? Scampi in the basket? Izaak's Delight? Walton's Surprise? Breambasher's Brunch? *Truite à l'Izaak*? What's that? Local trout, eh?

That'll do. Local trout. Fresh in today. Nothing like the old trout, straight from the water. And your wife cooks them herself, landlord? Can't be bad...

Within minutes, along comes the trout. Straight from the water – along with five thousand others at the trout farm – only a couple of months ago. Fresh in today from the local High Class Frozen Food Emporium. Home-cooked: microwaved to a turn in the good old-fashioned way. Tasting of traditional, hand-made, high quality cardboard. Can't whack it.

That's better. Feeling full now. A game or two on the fishing video machine, just to keep the old reflexes sharpened up. And then some fishing chat with newly-arrived fellow wallies. You've not a lot to say about the day's fishing, really, even though that gudgeon did fight like a tiger. But plenty to say about past triumphs.

Salmon? Yerss... Nothing like the thrill of the old salmon's first rush when you think you've hooked an express train. And the way the arms ache after playing it for an hour. Don't hold with having it gaffed by the ghillie, though. Much prefer to see the whole thing through alone. Takes more skill, of course, but at least when you've got the fish you know you've got it.

Another pint of the old Nutbrown, please, landlord. Slips down a treat, this stuff.

And sea trout. Say what you like about salmon, and you'd be the last to decry the fighting qualities of the King of Fish, but there's nothing like getting stuck in to the first run of sea trout. And the feeling of achievement and the glow of wellbeing after a day striding over the heather and stalking the run upriver...

Not that you've ever caught a salmon. Nor would you know a sea trout from a kipper if the kipper weren't brown and split down the middle. And striding over the heather for even half a day would leave you far too knackered for any glow of wellbeing to creep in.

OK, so the stories are a bit apocryphal (i.e. lies). But as a wally among wallies, you've got to keep your end up. And you did know somebody whose brother's mate caught a salmon once. So what the hell?

Another one of those, please, landlord. The old Nutnuts. Thirsty work, trying to outshout half a dozen fellow wallies in full spate.

At last the landlord calls time. Changing as he does so from the pleasant, rubicund and rustic mine host into a cockney gauleiter on attachment to the National Temperance League. Right, you lot! Ain't you got no 'omes to go to? Bloody fishermen... all the same. Let's have your glasses now, PLEASE!

Exit, stage left. Pausing only to call in the loo and throw up. Not that Old Izaak's Nutbrown Country Ale was over-strong. A specific gravity slightly lower than Pepsi, if anything. Bit fizzy, though, once it got down there. And somehow it didn't agree with the local trout. Fresh in today. Pity it was fresh out so soon.

But you can't have everything. Nice pub, that. Bit of atmosphere for a change. And interesting company. Must try it again some time...

123

Our Glorious Heritage

Fishing is not the only sport that brings people into contact with the joys of the countryside. There are other traditional country sports as well: fox hunting, stag hunting, hare coursing.

These other sports are under threat from a politically motivated, anarchistic rabble who seem to find something wrong in chasing intelligent and highly-developed mammals into exhaustion and a painful death.

Undermining our cherished British institutions, these people are. Attacking our traditional way of life. Curtailing our freedom. And if these sports are abolished, will not angling be next?

It's plain to see what we've lost already: bull-baiting, bear baiting, badger-baiting, otter hunting, cock-fighting; all sources of good wholesome fun. Even the outlawing of the humble rat pit meant the loss of innocent enjoyment for thousands of decent British sportsmen. Therefore we have to make a stand.

Angling can hold its head high. Its organisations have done a lot over recent years to make things easier on the fish. Young anglers are educated as a matter of course to be kind to the catch and to return the fish to the water unharmed at the end of the day.

Having learned all this, they may question the morality of other country sports. So we must explain to the kids that foxes rather enjoy the thrill of the chase, that hares are not *really* pulled limb from limb while they're still alive, and that clapped-out stags are quite relieved to have their throats cut in the middle of West Country holiday resorts.

It's very wally to Support Your Local Hunt. To stand outside the boozer on a crisp early morning, watching the mounted huntsmen knocking back the stirrup cups provided by the landlord, though the pub itself is closed to the local peasantry.

It's even wallier to put the spare change from your redundancy money into the hat being passed around to help the hunt carry on in the manner in which it's accustomed. To give a rousing, 'Good luck, sir!' as the hunt moves off, perhaps tugging the forelock as a sign of respect.

Don't whatever you do, step out into the road and wave, or greet the hunt with wild gesticulations. Nor stand there blowing a hunting horn and shouting, 'Yoiks!'. One would spook the horses and the other would confuse the hounds. For either, you are likely to be ridden down as a hunt saboteur.

The hunt is really grateful for your support. Gratified to see the displays of solidarity that bind true sportsmen together. After a hard day at the Stock Exchange, the MFH may even make time to visit your club and make a speech of thanks and an impassioned appeal for even closer unity among lovers of the countryside. Great bloke, the MFH. Just like one of us.

The comradeship may call for a few minor changes in your outlook. You may find yourself bursting into *Land of Hope and Glory*, bemoaning the loss of India and campaigning for the return of capital punishment.

Your vocabulary will be affected too, as you find yourself declaiming, 'Plenty of work about. No respect for authority. Bloody scroungers. Make more on the dole. Spend all their time in the pub.' All of which sentiments go down very well among your peers at the Job Centre.

Still, by now you've wallied yourself into a white heat of enthusiasm for our Great British traditions, and wish to make closer contact.

If you're a really serious wally, you will have scoured the jumble sales for old fox furs and will have at least one brush dangling from the aerial of your Mini. You'll have mounted the fox's mask tastefully on the bonnet, or perhaps stuck it as a Davy Crockett hat on the pike skull already glued there.

If the hounds pick up the scent of long-dead fox through the mothballs and try to drag the trophies from your transport, scratching the paintwork to ribbons in the process, don't try and kick them away. This would upset the huntsmen, who are very sensitive about the treatment of hounds and horses, and you may get a sound thrashing with a riding crop or, if you're lucky, a good old traditional all-British horsewhipping.

They'll apologise when they discover their mistake. They're nothing if not polite. But if you think you're getting an invitation to the Hunt Ball, or will even be allowed across the threshold of their local pub, forget it.

Wallies, they can do without. They've got enough of their own.

Beyond The Pale

To be an angling wally, you do not necessarily have to be an angler. You can become an Honorary Wally, an angling groupie, one of the many waterside wanderers for whom anglers and their doings have an irresistible fascination.

It is rarely that an angler gets through a day without being accosted by one or more of them. If he were to trek alone for weeks to a remote lake in the farthest reaches of the Andes, he wouldn't escape. Within minutes a lone figure would appear over the next peak, walk in a bee-line straight for him, sit down behind him and say, 'Mornin'...'

So why not become an Honorary Wally? It costs absolutely nothing, takes little experience, allows you to spend all your spare time in the open air, and you get told to bugger off by the most interesting people.

To help with your choice, here follows a catalogue of the best-known groupies. If you're not among these, don't fret. The list is open-ended and there's always room for another nutter.

Sorry. Nutter is too strong a word. It's not as if you were actually an angler, for God's sake. No, you're more of a – what's the word?

Nutter. That's the word.

MISTER LONELY

Mister Lonely is perhaps the easiest to become. You wander up behind an angler, sit down, and open with the immortal words, 'I really don't know how you've got the patience...'

For this one, ideally, you ought to be recently retired or newly redundant. You've been under the wife's feet all day, every day, for several weeks and finally she's told you she'd prefer your room to your company. It's not good to feel unwanted.

'Patience, yerss... How you can sit there all day just drowning worms is beyond me. I've always been so active, myself. Personally. Quick, you know. Never still a minute. The devil makes work for idle hands, I always say.

'Course, it takes all sorts. Some people just don't like work. Some people can sit around all day doing nothing. Still, if they like that sort of thing, good luck to them I say.

'Don't misunderstand me. I wasn't inferring that you were one of them. No, you look more the philosophical type. Like to think, if you take my meaning. Get away from it all. Peace and quiet, eh? Nothing like it, I always say. Bit of time to yourself.

'Or are you one of those who's just getting away from the wife? Is that it? Can't say I blame you. Some women take some living with. Course, my wife, she's a gem. Wouldn't be without her. Suppose everybody can't be that lucky...

'Go where? And do what? No need to take that attitude, old man. Only trying to make a bit of polite conversation. If I was ten years younger – And the same to you!

'Bloody cheek. No respect these days...'

MISTER KNOWALL

To become Mister Knowall involves a bit more homework, but at least you know that you're performing a service. Giving the novice angler the benefit of your years of experience, even though you don't do much fishing these days. Not since '53, anyway. Or was it '47?

Settling yourself comfortably at the top of the bank, you

'None of my business really, old son...'

observe the angler for a few minutes. After he's made a couple of casts and reeled in without result, you attract his attention by a sharp intake of breath.

'Tssk, tssk. None of my business really, old son, but I don't think you'll get anywhere like that. Not with worms on this stretch of bank. Cheese is the thing here. Always has been.

'What's your rod? Fourteen-footer. Ten's your top length here, old lad. Fourteen's much too cumbersome. And I see you've been going for that stretch under the willow over there. With respect, I don't think you'll do much there at all. If I were you, I'd try just downstream of those weeds.

'Not that this is a good spot to start with. Only an idiot would fish here, if you'll pardon my saying so. Over there's your spot... where that chap's just reeling in – a nice one, too, by the look of it.

'Not got much to say for yourself, have you? I mean, if I'm in the way, old son, just say the word. Only trying to help. That's what we're all here for.'

The angler breaks his silence with a 'Sod off!', hissed through clenched teeth. Your remonstrations at his incivility are cut short by the arrival of a steward. He points out that you are sitting at a match peg, frog-marches you away, then disqualifies the angler for talking.

The angler pursues you along the bank, slaps a well-soaked loaf in your face and wraps a rod rest around your neck. But how were you to know that the piece of wood with a number on it was a match peg?

Funny, that. Seven always used to be your lucky number...

THE DOG'S BEST FRIEND

An honorary wally's nuisance value increases considerably with a little help from the wally's best friend – the wallydog.

You can choose one from the selection in 'All in the Family' or get a common-or-garden mutt and train it up yourself. With proper training it is possible to combine the attributes of all the wallydogs into a single animal.

Put its suitability to the test with the Instant Obedience routine. Sit it on a hot stove and command firmly, 'Off!' If it stays there, looking hot and bothered but wagging its tail, you've found your dog.

As walker of a wallydog, you must dress the part. Tweeds are the thing, topped off by a deerstalker or pork pie hat. Carry a stout, ash walking stick, knobbly for preference, and wear a pair of sturdy brogues. All this makes it look to the angler as if you know about dogs, as if that thing by your side is under control. By the time he's realised his mistake, it's too late.

Stop by him for the old social chit-chat. Nice day for the time of year ... bit nippy first thing, though ... how's your luck? ... all that sort of stuff. Meanwhile, your dog:

Flushes every living thing from the undergrowth for a hundred yards around;

Scratches all the turf off the bank around the angler, leaving the place looking like an end-of-season penalty area;

Charges madly around in ever-decreasing circles, but fails to make the ultimate tight turn which would solve everybody's problem;

Digs under the angler's basket;

Eats his groundbait;

Dives in the water, swims around for a while, savages the odd duck, and on the way back bites the rod tip in two;

Shakes itself on the bank, soaking the angler to the skin;

As an afterthought, pees up his leg.

You reluctantly make your farewells as the angler wrestles the dog on the bank in an attempt to retrieve his lunch packet. Few anglers win this contest and some of them get quite peeved about it.

Beware the more subtle anglers who, on being pestered

for a sandwich ask, 'Hey – is it OK if I throw your dog a bit?' On being given the go-ahead, they'll pick the thing up and throw it a bit – twenty-five yards down the towpath.

BOOTLACE BIKINI

Here we have one of the truly amazing phenomena of the wallygroupie scene. The Bootlace Bikini.

Why she happens, why of all things she should be keenly interested in anglers and angling, nobody knows. Those anglers who have endeavoured to plumb the depths of the mystery have disappeared without trace.

Some of the manifestations, admittedly, are all in the mind. The average angler, sitting hunched and staring at his float, is not sunk deep in concentration. He is suffering from sensory deprivation or the effects of the Demon Drink, both of which are notorious for bringing about such primordial and atavistic – i.e. randy – hallucinations such as a nubile maiden appearing from nowhere.

There's even a commercial use of the vision. In match angling, every split-second counts. Every twitch of the float could mean another ounce to set towards the individual and team weights. And it is not unknown for unscrupulous persons, such as the opposition, or free-lance punters with bets on the result, to persuade with filthy lucre, i.e. money, a nubile maiden to walk the opposite bank in a state of undress. Well, not quite undress, but not enough dress to make any difference. Enough to put anyone off the next twitch of the float, apart from the Mad Matchman who doesn't count because he's barmy anyway.

But she does exist. Headbanging, sex obsession, alcohol poisoning and commercial exploitation apart. We're talking about the genuine Bootlace Bikini who appears in the flesh to quite normal, sober, sane and uncompetitive anglers. Innocent and trusting and wear-

At this point it is best to leave . . .

ing just enough to cover her confusion.

She's a specialised groupie, and to become one you need a few basic qualifications: female, under twenty-five, in good fettle, big knockers and only one head.

By the very act of approaching a quite normal, uncompetitive, happily married angler, you qualify immediately as an Honorary Wally. But beware: the normal, uncompetitive, happily married angler is not made of stone. Be prepared for reactions not normally associated with the pursuit of the angle.

Your usual approach is made from behind. Silently. The angler is not aware of your presence until he feels an unaccustomed heat on the back of his neck. This is caused either by the reflection of the sun on your lily white torso or the giving-out of heat from your nutbrown frame after you've spent a morning getting tanned.

His first reaction is often less than civil.

'What the bloody –'

But once he claps eyes on you, this changes to a simple and strangled, 'Errrhhh... Aaarrrhhh...' Perhaps followed by such traditional angling phrases as, 'At last, my luck has changed,' or 'I should live so long...'

'Hello,' you say.

'Hell*ooo*,' he says.

'I'm so interested in fishing,' you say. 'Please tell me all about it.'

'Aaarrgh,' he says. 'Well, what you do is to put this... phwarh... on to this here... cripes... and then cast out like... jeez... Once the float's settled in the water you wait for a knocker – knock... Sort of bum – boom-boom – it goes. And then you lift the rod a tit – a bit – and get stuck in. Aaaarrrrghhhh...'

At this point in the demonstration you become aware of some angling techniques seldom mentioned in the instruction books or the specialist press. He picks up a handful of worms and stuffs them in his mouth; puts a cigarette in his ear and lights his nose; sticks a whole cheese sandwich on the end of his hook and casts it into the trees on the opposite bank. His hair stands on end, his eyes go funny, his rod tip trembles and his specs steam up.

At this point it is best to leave. He's told you all he knows, or wants to know, about fishing, and his blood pressure is turning critical.

Noble people, fishermen. So cool. So calm. So stolid. So self-controlled.

P.S. Excuse wobbly writing.

Some Side-Splitting WallyJapes: 4

It is not unknown for anglers to be a bit adrift towards the end of an evening, the frustrations of the sport being what they are and the connection between angling and the Demon Drink being what it is.

Should a mate be in the condition known to medical science as tight as a newt, pissed as a pudden, legless, stonkers or ratarsed, it is incumbent upon you to see the lad safely back to his Nearest and Dearest.

It will take two or more of you to see him home. There is no way that one man can support two sets of tackle plus a mate who is protesting, singing, weeping or comatose.

Here is the perfect opportunity for one of the most popular of wallyjapes: knocking at the door and running away. But with a little extra preparation you can have several variations on the basic theme; each guaranteed to get him further into dead lumber or confined to the doghouse for a month.

By the time you get him home he is usually in too feeble a state to protest, if not actually out to the wide. The basic jape is to lean him against the front door, knock and run. But take care with the preparation. Lean him against the door only; tuck in his arms so that he gains no support from either side. Drape his tackle around him so that the whole shoot falls in with him.

Do not run away immediately. If his Ever Loving failed to hear the knocking or ringing, he would simply snooze the night away and be roused by the milkman. So, after raising the alarm, wait at least until you see or hear signs of activity; lights going on, footsteps on the stairs or tinkling female tones enquiring, 'And where the hell do you think *you've* been until this time?' Better still, if you can bear it, wait until you see the reds of her eyes. Then run.

As the door is flung open wide and angrily, as it usually is, he will cant from his upright position and fall flat on his face, or back as the case may be, landing comatose in the hall in a welter of tackle and leftover bait.

From there he is either dragged up the hall and left to spend the night at the bottom of the stairs, to be dealt with in greater detail on the morrow, or belaboured unmercifully with a blunt instrument. Often both.

It is not unknown for the Nearest and Dearest to go through his pockets in an attempt to discover how he came to be in this state. In anticipation of this you can use Variation Number One: the 'Eek!' Variation. Fill his pockets with leftover maggots, worms, bits of squid or ripe rubbydubby. Discovery of this brings an immediate reaction, which you'll be able to hear from your hiding place at the other end of the street.

More subtle and even wallier is Variation Number Two; the 'Dirty Dog' variation. Just slip into his pockets a few articles of female apparel such as bra, knickers or tights, and give him a few squirts of perfume to arouse the suspicions of his trusting wife. You have to wait a little longer for the reaction, but it's worth it when it comes.

You may not see your mate for a month or six weeks after the jape, depending on how long it takes for the swellings to go down or the plaster to be taken off.

If you're lucky, he may not remember who took him home. If you're unlucky, it may be your turn for the intensive care unit.

Bump In The Night

Angling is one of the few pastimes in which you can leave
home all day, all night, even a whole weekend, for an
unspecified destintion and no questions asked. So you
may as well make the most of it with a spot of
nightfishing.

The right gear is essential. A sturdy and waterproof
tent, big enough for four. Groundsheet, airbed, double
sleeping bag. (Double sleeping bag? When the tent takes
four? Hang on: all will be revealed.) Scotch, gin, vodka,
mixers. Ghetto blaster. Miss Maisie Fruit.

That's it: all the essentials.

Get to the waterside as dusk is falling. Pitch tent. Lay
groundsheet. Blow up airbed, arrange sleeping bag.
Arrange scotch, gin, vodka, mixers and ghetto blaster
near to hand. Arrange Maisie Fruit likewise.

Bait? Fishing tackle? What do you think this is? Some
kind of wallyouting? No, nightfishing, this is. Fishing
tackle! What next?

Now, where were we? Scotch, gin, vodka, mixers.
Maisie Fruit...

*   *   *

Don't despair. You can turn nightfishing into a wallyouting before you can say, 'Bottoms up'.

There will be the odd genuine nightfisher about.
Crouched shivering over his rod, eyes fixed on the bite

indicator or on the luminous float; spartan tent behind him holding nothing but a sleeping bag (single), packet of butties and thermos of Bovril. Give him a treat.

Let the ghetto blaster liven up the night with some good old discosound, a spot of wallysoul and the latest heavy metal. Not only will it help to get Maisie Fruit in the mood, it'll drown her maidenly squeals once she's in it. (By which time you will appreciate the advantages of a four-man tent. In a tent made for two, there's seldom room to swing a cat. Let alone Miss Maisie Fruit.)

When she's got enough gin and vodka down her, having gone steady on the mixers, she might fancy a jog along the bank; hurdling the genuine nightfisher's rods when she can see them; falling flat on her shock absorbers when she can't, After that, the pair of you might fancy a spot of skinnydipping, just the thing for sobering up and putting down the cruising carp.

The genuine nightfishers, being the selfish and mean-minded spoilsports that they are, might attempt to cut short the skinnydipping by casting a few pike spoons in your general direction. Or perhaps take more drastic action such as burning your tent down. Make the most of the warmth from the blaze: as you left your clothes in there, you'll finish up with your ardour decidedly cooled.

That could be a problem next morning. Arriving home and having to explain to the wife. The tent going up in flames? Sheer accident. Could happen to anybody. But how come you're starkers? And why is that pike wobbler dangling from your bum?

Wallying To The End

After all the time and trouble you've put into becoming a
wallyangler, it would seem only right and proper that you
should get some reward. Although the pursuit of
wallyness is mainly an amateur sport, it is possible to
turn professional and make a bob or two – even a living –
out of it. Take, for instance, the Tellywally.

The commercial tellywally appears often in television
adverts for unwholesome or wally-orientated products
which need a wholesome and wally image.

There he is by the water, using a fly rod and line with
float-ledger terminal tackle. A fine figure of a man:
bronzed, handsome, well-muscled, sober, and not knowing the first thing about what he's supposed to be doing.

There's his float dipping madly, being pulled underwater by an invisible but very damp production assistant.
He strikes – and he's into a whopper (played by the same
damp production assistant). Out comes the fish (played
by an unrecognisable species, possibly saltwater and
very probably dead).

All of this is to encourage you to: eat chocolate bars
which make you fat and rot your teeth; take out life
insurance; bank with somebody who has only your
interests at heart. (Until you run up an overdraft, that is,
but they leave that bit out.)

You can be a commercial familywally, taking your
impossibly clean and appealing kids down to the water on
a summer morning. For this it is essential to be

sickeningly cheerful, to wear a fluorescent pullover that would scare every fish for miles, and to be incredibly hearty. You spend some time hailing other familywallies as they too move down to the water with their own impossibly clean and appealing kids.

After a highly exciting and fun-packed ten seconds on the bank, you return in an even more sickeningly cheerful mood, with the kids impossibly cleaner and even more appealing, to tuck into a plateful of cereal with not a lot of food value. The tucking-in is presided over by a wife-and-mother wallyperson who looks at the whole bunch of you adoringly and indulgently. You return the adoring and indulgent gaze – a masterpiece of the actor's art, as in real life you'd be playing hell because she was too bone-idle to whip up a decent breakfast.

You can, if you prefer, be the newtownwally, who rises at dawn and, after a six-second cycle ride on futuristic and traffic-free flyovers, has progressed from the centre of a new town to a water set in idyllic countryside.

During the ride, you are not called upon to be arrested for cycling on the motorway, are not knocked off your bike by a juggernaut, do not find your route obstructed by the footings for another thousand houses. The water is not grossly polluted from the building work, nor has it been filled in to provide the site for an atomic power station. No, there it is, limpid in the morning mist and full of fish, as can be deduced from the way your float bobs sharply half a second after being cast in.

Another source of tellywally income is to appear as frontwally on programmes about country pursuits. For these it is necessary to wander through half an hour of telly time, extolling the virtues of the country life, supping a pint or two of Old Izaak's Nutbrown Country Ale while chatting up the landlord of a wallypub, patting a horse or two, and finally getting down to flicking a fly line over a private water, way beyond the means of most of your audience.

The programme ends with the catching of a trout,

which you unskilfully beat to death with an under-weighted priest as the end credits roll, unaware that in so doing you are putting most of your viewers off fishing for life.

*   *   *

Not only do old wallies never die, they're very reluctant even to fade away. You can drink for free throughout your dotage by becoming an Oldest Inhabitant.

For this you need to be an incredibly clean or an incredibly dirty old man, and to find a country pub whose landlord is willing to let you sit in the chimney seat and chat up visiting anglers.

You are not exactly cadging drinks: you are providing an information and archive service, dispensing wisdom and advice in return for pints of Old Izaak's Nutbrown Country Ale or, if you're wallying in the West Country, Old Izaak's Piscatorial Scrumpy.

There are three main types of information you can offer: Old Country Lore, Secret Baits, and Memories of the Dear Dead Days. None of this need be strictly accurate; in fact it can be a load of old twaddle. So long as it's what potential wallies want to hear, who's going to complain?

Old Country Lore is mainly about the weather:

'Arr, Young Zurr. If 'ee wants to know when rain be due, just watch the animals. If 'ee zees a cow lyin' down, if 'ee 'ears a donkey brayin', or zees birds flyin' early 'ome to roost, we're in for rain all roight. Mark my words.'

Probably a townie, Young Zurr will be unaware that cows lie down when they're tired or dead, that donkeys bray when they're sexed-up – which is roughly every ten minutes – and that birds fly home to roost because they've had enough and fancy a kip.

Secret Baits have to be difficult to come by:

'My old dad used to swear by greaves, Young Zurr. Deadly, it were. Oh arr, and the pith from a two-year-old bullock. And for barbel down yon bottom stretch, worms.

By the sack, mind. No use messing about with ones and twos.'

It's not been easy – i.e. almost impossible – to get greaves for the past 50 years. Should Young Zurr ask for bullocks' pith in a supermarket, he'll be arrested and charged with lisping likely to cause a breach of the peace. And by the time he's dug a sackful of worms, he will be too exhausted to lift a rod.

The Dear Dead Days routine is easy: just a Cider-with-Rosie ramble down Memory Lane. About the gentry at the Big House. About the punts on the river and the gudgeon fries on summer evenings. About rides on the haywains down to the water. About the immense catches of fish that, alas, are no longer possible these days. About how well you remember the capture of that huge stuffed pike over the mantelpiece.

Be careful with the pike story. If Young Zurr were to rub the dust off the plaque, he might be amazed to discover that you are 172 years old.

Some Uses For A Dead Wally

Death comes to us all in the end. To a wallyangler it can come sooner than later: living, as he does, life to the full, and often in the company of fellow wallies, whose own actions may have hastened his demise.

Sad as the departure of a wallyangler is, especially if he owed you a bob or two, his usefulness is not over. Though he may have shuffled off this mortal coil, he can still be of service for a while to his fellow man. It's as he would have wished.

The first thing to do, on his keeling over, is to ascertain that he is in fact dead; not just dozed off or suffering from an overdose of the hard stuff.

If it happens on the bank, shout into his ear, 'Hey up! Your float's just dipped!' or 'Quick – it's the bailiff!'

In the absence of a response, try, 'Phwarh! Look at that little darlin' over there! She's just dived in starkers!'

With still no reponse, try the ultimate receptivity tests, 'Fancy a scotch?'. Or, 'Come on – they're open!'

If he fails to react even to that, there's not much more you can do short of lighting a fire under him, but there are regulations about that sort of thing on the bank.

The main thing is not to waste him. Prop him up on his basket with his second-best rod in his hand. You can use his best one, as well as the rest of his bait and any full bottles he has about his person.

Not only can you now fish his swim as well as your own, you have a ready answer for the bailiff when he asks for the tickets – 'He's got 'em.'

144

Though it is very bad form for anyone to pop his clogs in a pub, especially if he hasn't bought a round, it is sometimes unavoidable. But it must not be allowed to cloud the evening's jollifications.

The first thing to do is drink his beer. As he would have wished. You can shove him under the table until time is called and the crib game is finished, but this is less than imaginative and unworthy of wallycompany.

Use him instead to keep the place at the bar; sit him against the window to keep the draught out; or have beer for the assembled company put on the slate and tell the landlord, 'Our friend over there will settle up'.

Now and again a wallyangler will pass on in the middle of a club committee meeting. There's not a lot of use you can make of him there, except to nudge his elbow for the casting vote. Deaths at committee meetings generally go unnoticed anyway, there being little difference in appearance between the Dear Departed and the other members.

* * *

Now comes the hardest part: breaking the news to his Ever Loving. It has to be done tactfully, and there are several recommended wallyways of breaking it gently. Such as:
'Am I addressing the Widow Wally?'

*

'I'm sorry to tell you that your husband's best fishing hat has been ruined.'
    'But he wasn't wearing his best fishing hat.'
    'That's lucky, then, because a tree's just fallen on it.'

*

'A whisky vat burst in the distillery and spilled its contents into the canal. I'm sorry to tell you that your husband was overcome by fumes, fell in the water and drowned.'

'Oh, dear. Was it painful?'

'I don't think so. He got out three times for a pee.'

*

And then there was the telegram from Australia: REGRET WALLY KILLED WHILE FISHING. WHAT ARE YOUR WISHES?

Reply from wife: SEND HIM HOME. JUST AS HE IS.

A little while later, further telegram from wife: MUST BE SOME MISTAKE. ONLY SHARK IN COFFIN.

Reply from Australia: NO MISTAKE. WALLY IN SHARK. JUST AS HE WAS.

*

Tact, of course, must always be the watchword, and all personal considerations must be put aside. Do not make the mistake of the man who knocked at the door and asked, 'Is Wally in?'

The woman who answered burst into tears and said, 'I'm sorry to have to tell you that my husband passed away only half an hour ago.'

'I *am* sorry,' said his mate. 'Did he say anything about a bait tin?'

*   *   *

All that remains is the selection of an epitaph for the headstone: something which expresses appropriate sympathy and gives some indication of the way the deceased came by his untimely end. The following may be found useful:

Poor old Wally.
He didn't know

That when you dropped anchor
You had to let go.

*

The reason Wally's
No longer here
Was a very long walk
On a very short pier.

*

Here lies O'Wally
From Liffeydownlug.
His boat disappeared
When he pulled out the plug.

*

Here lies Wally.
He would have stayed longer.
But he tried to wrestle
A nine-foot-six conger.

*

There wasn't much of Wally
When we laid him on the deck.
A shark had bitten his big toe off
Right up to the neck.

*

Thank you. And goodnight. May I leave you with the wallywish that the biggest you've had will be the smallest you'll get. Or words to that effect.

The Book Of
ROYAL
LISTS

CRAIG BROWN & LESLEY CUNLIFFE

**What should you serve the Royal Family if they
drop in for dinner?
How does the Queen keep her Corgies content?
Which clergyman did Prince Charles throw into
the fountain at Balmoral?
What are Princess Diana's favourite sweets?
Which television programmes does the Queen
Mother like best?
How can you recognise a Royal racing pigeon?**

The Royal Family is no ordinary family, and Royal Lists
are not like ordinary lists. Here at last are the answers to
all the questions that have intrigued dedicated Royal-
watchers, loyal patriots, convinced monarchists and the
millions of adoring fans around the world who follow
every move of Britain's first family.

THE BOOK OF ROYAL LISTS is the most
comprehensive collection of information ever assembled
about the British Royal Family and their ancestors.
Witty and informed, amusing but respectful, it surprises,
charms and dazzles.

HUMOUR   0 7221 1934 8   £2.50

ROBERT K. G. TEMPLE

DID YOU KNOW THAT . . .

There may be two suns in the solar system!

Canaries lose a fifth of their brains in the winter – but get it all back in the spring!

The lesbian whiptail lizards of America clone their offspring!

There are planets in our galaxy which are 17% crystallized diamonds!

Some birds have a fear of flying!

STRANGE THINGS:

a bizarre, baffling and mind-boggling guide to the quirks of nature, including . . . heavy-breathing water lilies, sun-tanned eggs, irate embryos, perfumed moths, sensitive sponges, mathematical monkeys, over-sexed fruitflies and many other wonders.

SCIENCE   0 7221 8410 7   £1.50

A selection of bestsellers from **SPHERE**

FICTION

MANDARIN	Robert Elegant	£2.95 ☐
POSSESSIONS	Judith Michael	£3.95 ☐
KING OF HEAVEN	Burt Hirschfeld	£1.95 ☐
MAN OF WAR	John Masters	£2.50 ☐
FIREFOX DOWN	Craig Thomas	£2.25 ☐

FILM & TV TIE-INS

INDIANA JONES AND THE GIANTS OF THE SILVER TOWER	R. L. Stine	£1.25 ☐
INDIANA JONES AND THE EYE OF THE FATES	Richard Wenk	£1.25 ☐
MINDER – BACK AGAIN	Anthony Masters	£1.50 ☐
SUPERGIRL	Norma Fox Mazer	£1.75 ☐

NON-FICTION

THE FASTEST DIET	Rosie Boycott	£1.25 ☐
THE HYPOCHONDRIAC'S HANDBOOK	Doctors Lee Schreiner and George Thomas	£1.50 ☐
THE ULTIMATE COCKTAIL BOOK	M. C. Martin	£1.95 ☐

All Sphere books are available at your local bookshop or newsagent, or can be ordered direct from the publisher. Just tick the titles you want and fill in the form below.

Name_____

Address_____

_____

Write to Sphere Books, Cash Sales Department, P.O. Box 11, Falmouth, Cornwall TR10 9EN
Please enclose a cheque or postal order to the value of the cover price plus:
UK: 45p for the first book, 20p for the second book and 14p per copy for each additional book ordered to a maximum charge of £1.63.
OVERSEAS: 75p for the first book plus 21p per copy for each additional book.
BFPO & EIRE: 45p for the first book, 20p for the second book plus 14p per copy for the next 7 books, thereafter 8p per book.

Sphere Books reserve the right to show new retail prices on covers which may differ from those previously advertised in the text or elsewhere, and to increase postal rates in accordance with the PO.